New Orleans Sketches

WILLIAM

FAULKNER:

New Orleans Sketches

EDITED BY *Carvel Collins*

RANDOM HOUSE, New York

PUBLISHER'S NOTE

The text of this edition has been corrected in the
light of new evidence and completely reset. An
additional essay, "Sherwood Anderson" (1925),
has been included as an Appendix. *First printing*

Library of Congress Catalog Card Number: 68-14495

Manufactured in the United States of America
98765

Preface

M<small>R. GEORGE W. HEALY, JR.,</small> Managing Editor of the New Orleans *Times-Picayune*, generously gave permission in 1950 to reprint William Faulkner's sketches after I had found sixteen of them which that newspaper had published twenty-five years before. Soon, however, admirers of Faulkner at the University of Minnesota, coming upon some of the sketches, brought out eleven of them as *Mirrors of Chartres Street by William Faulkner*. After the two additional signed *Times-Picayune* sketches in the "Mirrors" series were pointed out to the Minnesota editors, they published them as a second book: *Jealousy and Episode: Two Stories by William Faulkner*. Thus thirteen of the sixteen sketches had been brought back into print in two volumes; but three signed sketches, one of them among the most significant, still remained in the old file of the newspaper. When collation showed that the texts of the two volumes of reprintings were garbled, it seemed proper to put together all sixteen sketches in one volume with, hopefully, a somewhat more accurate text. And it seemed well to include, with the generous permission of Mrs. Lillian Friend Marcus, Managing Editor of *The Double Dealer*, a reprinting of "New Orleans," the group of very short sketches which

Faulkner had published in 1925 in that New Orleans literary magazine and which, though republished in 1932 with Faulkner's permission by the prescient Paul Romaine in his now rare volume *Salmagundi*, were no longer in print.

The resulting book was brought out by the Rutgers University Press in 1957 as *William Faulkner: New Orleans Sketches*. It has since appeared in an edition by Grove Press and in several editions in Europe.

Revising the book for the present edition has made possible the insertion of corrections which Faulkner himself fortunately made in the text of "New Orleans." This edition also incorporates textual changes which Mr. William B. Wisdom of New Orleans kindly has suggested as a result of his comparison of the *Double Dealer* text of "New Orleans" with Faulkner's original typescript, now in Mr. Wisdom's highly significant Faulkner collection, for the generous use of which I am extremely grateful.

This edition contains an additional essay, "Sherwood Anderson," which Faulkner wrote in 1925 for the Dallas *Morning News* out of his recently formed association with Anderson at New Orleans. It is reprinted here as an appendix, with the kind permission of the staff of the Dallas *News;* of Professor James B. Meriwether, who first reprinted it in 1957 in *The Princeton University Library Chronicle;* and of Dr. William S. Dix, Librarian of Princeton University. For information about the relationship between Sherwood Anderson and Faulkner in New Orleans, I am especially indebted to Mrs. Elizabeth Prall Anderson, Mrs. Lillian Friend Marcus, Mr. Ben Wasson, the late Messrs. John McClure, Julius Weis Friend, and Phil Stone, and the late Mrs. John McClure. For help while reading in the Sherwood Anderson papers at the Newberry Library in Chicago, I am grateful to that Library's generous and effective staff, particularly Mr. William Towner, Director, and Mrs. Amy Nyholm.

The late Mr. William Spratling not only answered questions out of his friendship and collaboration with Faulkner but generously gave permission to reproduce a portrait drawing. Mr. Carl Petersen has repeatedly made available the combined excellence of his knowledge of Faulkner and his collection of materials by and about him. Mr. Paul Romaine, who early sensed the high quality of Faulkner's art, has been at all times open-handed with documents and clear answers to confused questions.

In this edition the introduction, which discusses Faulkner and the sketches, has been revised in the light of additional information from former acquaintances of Faulkner and from documents which I have been allowed to read since the appearance of the first version. To the various owners of those documents, who have asked to remain unnamed, I give my thanks, as well as to the scores of people who generously have been willing to recall their associations with William Faulkner at New Orleans.

I also thank Mr. William Sloane, Miss Helen Stewart, and their colleagues at the Rutgers University Press for the kindness with which they have permitted the publication of this edition; and Mr. Albert Erskine of Random House for his help in its preparation.

C. C.

University of Notre Dame
November, 1967

Contents

Contents

Introduction

In 1925 at the age of twenty-seven William Faulkner, who had been almost exclusively a poet, began to publish fiction. During that year, in which he lived for six months at New Orleans, he contributed a group of sketches to a New Orleans literary magazine, *The Double Dealer*, and sixteen signed stories and sketches to the Sunday feature section of the New Orleans *Times-Picayune*.

He had ended one phase of his life shortly before he reached New Orleans: on October 31, 1924, he had resigned from his job as postmaster at the University of Mississippi. His three years spent in the post office had not been predominantly pleasant, and immediately after his resignation he had made his now famous remark about the relief of being no longer at the beck and call of everyone who, in that day of cheaper postage, had two cents. He also had seemed glad to be free to give full time to writing—free again, as he had told his friend Ben Wasson the day after he had resigned, to be outdoors watching the color of life, taking pipe and paper to dream and write. He had added in his comments to Wasson that he intended never again to be controlled by the clock or by the daily routine of conventional employment.

Another friend, Phil Stone, recalled that Faulkner had gone to New York before the post office job partly in order to be nearer publishers who might accept his poetry. With the postmastership ended, he had decided to go to Europe, in part perhaps, Phil Stone suggested, on the principle that one way to get literary recognition in the United States was to get it abroad, a principle which had already served Robert Frost—and much later was actually to serve Faulkner.

He may also have decided to go abroad in reaction to what he felt then was the low state of literary life in the United States, of which he spoke sharply in an essay published by the New Orleans *Double Dealer* almost as soon as he reached the city, saying that literary criticism was much better in England than in America:

> Of course there are in America critics as sane and tolerant and as soundly equipped, but with a few exceptions they have no status: the magazines which set the standard ignore them; or finding conditions unbearable, they ignore the magazines and live abroad. In a recent number of "The Saturday Review" Mr. Gerald Gould, reviewing "The Hidden Player" by Alfred Noyes, says:
> "People do not talk like that . . . It will not do to set down ordinary speech of ordinary people; that would generally be dull . . . To give the deadly detail is misleading." Here is the essential of criticism. So just and clear and complete: there is nothing more to be said. A criticism which not only the public, but the author as well, may read with profit. But what American critic would let it go at this? . . . The English review criticizes the book, the American the author. The

American critic foists upon the reading public a distorted buffoon within whose shadow the titles of sundry uncut volumes vaguely lurk. Surely, if there are two professions in which there should be no professional jealousy, they are prostitution and literature.

Whatever his reasons, Faulkner seems to have made clear as he left Oxford that he was leaving the country; for the author of a "Hayseed Letter" in the University of Mississippi student newspaper on December 5, 1924, had said that Faulkner had "done give up the post offise . . . It is rumored that Bill will retire to some tropic iland, lay in the sweet smelling locust leaves and gourd vines and indite sonnets to the pore helpless world, which no one can diagnose." The town newspaper had said, more soberly, "Reports are current that Mr. Falkner will go abroad in the near future." Additional evidence refuting the occasionally expressed opinion that Faulkner went to New Orleans with the intention of settling into the literary group surrounding Sherwood Anderson is in the review of his book *The Marble Faun*, which John McClure wrote for the *Times-Picayune* almost as soon as Faulkner reached New Orleans: "This reviewer believes that Mr. Faulkner promises fine things. He is soon off for Europe."

But he postponed his embarkation and began almost at once to write the sketches and stories which are reprinted here. Previously he had published two pieces of fiction—a story and a short sketch, both in the University of Mississippi student newspaper. He had tried his hand at drama in at least one unpublished college play and in *Marionettes*, which he "published" himself during 1920, hand-lettering the booklets, skillfully illustrating them somewhat after the manner of Aubrey Beardsley, and giving them to a few friends.

He had also written a large quantity of poetry: The earliest of his literary works which I have been able to identify is a poem—which he had written in 1918 for publication while he was in pilot training at Toronto. The next year he had published a poem in *The New Republic*. A poem of his had appeared in *The Double Dealer* in 1922, and many others in the annual and the newspaper of the University of Mississippi during his years there as student and as postmaster. He had prepared part of a volume of poems, then called *The Greening Bough*, which was to appear a decade later, and had just brought out, at the end of 1924, his first book of poetry, *The Marble Faun*, with an introduction by Phil Stone.

Though he must have felt some disappointment because his poetry was not being more widely published, he had kept his sense of humor: when *The New Republic*, which had accepted "L'Apres-Midi d'un Faune," had returned other poems, Faulkner and Stone as a joke had submitted a poem by John Clare without identifying its author. After it had been rejected, they had submitted "Kubla Khan" and had been amused when the editor, in returning that poem also, had said: I like it, Mr. Coleridge, but it doesn't seem to be getting anywhere.

Faulkner's poetry, published and unpublished, and his early critical essays show that he had been interested in the work of, among others, Shelley, Keats, Verlaine, Housman, Eliot, Pound—and Swinburne, whom he called, in a review for the college newspaper, "a mixture of passionate adoration of beauty and as passionate despair and disgust with its manifestations and accessories in the human race." Other reviews he wrote for the college paper showed his admiration for Conrad Aiken—a "rift of heaven sent blue"—as well as his disapproval of poetry by Vachel Lindsay and Carl Sandburg. Of Amy Lowell he wrote in 1921 that she "tried a polyphonic prose which, in spite of the fact that she had created some delightful statuettes of perfectly blown glass, is merely a literary flatulency."

Through the publication by *The Double Dealer* of his poem "Portrait" in 1922, while he was postmaster, William Faulkner had made his first slight connection with the literary life of New Orleans. When he reached the city three years later he found the magazine's office, in an old building at 204 Baronne Street, to be one of the focal points for the literary people of the city. And he found in one of its editors, John McClure, a man who would be an active sponsor and friend for many years. McClure's remarkably perceptive reviews were a feature of *The Double Dealer;* and his regular column, "Literature and Less," in the *Times-Picayune* made its Sunday issues outstanding among American newspapers which published book pages. McClure had been a force on *The Double Dealer* staff since its founding three years before Faulkner's arrival in New Orleans.

Among the magazine's authors were Sherwood Anderson, Hart Crane, John Crowe Ransom, Djuna Barnes, Robert Penn Warren, Maxwell Bodenheim, Carl Van Vechten, Hamilton Basso, Donald Davidson, Richard Aldington, Mark Van Doren, Ezra Pound, Malcolm Cowley, Thornton Wilder, Allen Tate, and Edmund Wilson. The editors and publishers of *The Double Dealer* were proud in later years that they early had printed the work

Introduction

of both Hemingway and Faulkner—so early, in fact, that
when a sketch by Hemingway appeared in May, 1922,
the magazine's notes on contributors said of him: "Ernest
M. Hemingway is a young American writer who lives in
Paris and enjoys the favor of Ezra Pound. He expects
shortly to bring out a book of poems."

One of *The Double Dealer* founders, Albert Gold-
stein, recalling that the magazine had been intended not
only to encourage new writers but to prove to H. L.
Mencken the error of his contention that the South was
without culture, has pointed out that it accomplished
both missions; for in its six years of existence it not only
established an admirable list of "firsts" among authors but
impressed Mencken enough for him to write in *The
Smart Set* that *The Double Dealer* was delivering the
South from a cultural swamp.

Examination of the issues of *The Double Dealer*
quickly makes clear that the people who ran it—with
whom William Faulkner associated in the early months
of 1925 and again in 1926 after he returned from Europe
—were extremely aware of the intellectual and aesthetic
currents which were making the twenties so important
in American literary history. And with our knowledge
of Faulkner's subsequent writing it is pleasant to read in
The Double Dealer a prophetic editorial, first published
in 1921 and republished in a 1924 memorial issue, in
which Basil Thompson, almost as though he could fore-
see Faulkner's career, said:

> It is high time, we believe, for some doughty, clear-
> visioned penman to emerge from the sodden marshes of
> Southern literature . . .
> It is no idle conceit to hazard that some Southern

Sherwood Anderson, some less tedious Sinclair Lewis, lurks even now in our midst . . . There are hundreds of little towns in Alabama, Mississippi and Louisiana fairly bubbling with the stuff of stories . . . The old Southern pot-boiler must go out—the lynching-bee, little Eva, Kentucky Colonel, beautiful Quadroon stuff —a surer, saner, more virile, less sentimental literature must come in. By all the symptoms the reaction is near at hand.

Sherwood Anderson was clearly the greatest celebrity in what Faulkner, years later, would call "our small New Orleans group." Early in 1922 Anderson had lived briefly in New Orleans, taking a room in the French Quarter and reporting that he had come to New Orleans "because I love something basically cultural in the life here, because there is published in this city the *Double Dealer*." He had gone on in the same essay to urge other artists to come to New Orleans:

> . . . I address these fellows. I want to tell them of long quiet walks to be taken on the levee in back-of-town, where old ships, retired from service, thrust their masts up into the evening sky. On the streets here the crowds have a more leisurely stride . . . I stick to my pronouncement that culture means first of all the enjoyment of life, leisure and a sense of leisure. It means time for a play of the imagination over the facts of life, it means time and vitality to be serious about really serious things and a background of joy in life in which to refresh the tired spirits.
>
> In a civilization where the fact becomes dominant, submerging the imaginative life, you will have what is dominant in the cities of Pittsburgh and Chicago today.
>
> When the fact is made secondary to the desire to live, to love, and to understand life, it may be that we will have in more American cities a charm of place

such as one finds in the older parts of New Orleans now.

In the summer of 1924, after Anderson had married Miss Elizabeth Prall, he had returned to New Orleans and settled with a feeling of permanence in the French Quarter, renting on the second floor of the upper Pontalba Building an apartment which he called a "grand place," overlooking Jackson Square.

Faulkner had first met Sherwood Anderson during a brief trip to New Orleans late in 1924. Visiting his friend Ben Wasson at Greenville, Mississippi, Faulkner had spoken of his great admiration for Anderson's volume of stories, *Horses and Men,* saying that Anderson's "I'm a Fool" and Conrad's *Heart of Darkness* were the two best stories he had ever read. When Faulkner had added that he would like to meet Anderson, Wasson had pointed out that Anderson was in New Orleans and that Faulkner already knew his wife, Elizabeth, for whom Faulkner had worked briefly in a New York bookstore before her marriage. Wasson had urged him to go to New Orleans and call at the Andersons' apartment. Faulkner had done so, and his introduction to Anderson had become the basis for Anderson's sketch "A Meeting South," which describes the first evening Anderson spent with a new acquaintance who is certainly Faulkner.

After a return to Oxford, Faulkner came again to New Orleans at the start of the new year, 1925, this time to look for passage on a boat to England. He became a guest in the Andersons' large Pontalba apartment. He was very happy there, appreciating Mrs. Anderson's concern for his welfare and enjoying the company of Anderson's son. Sherwood Anderson himself was away from New Orleans, lecturing in several states and writing in New York.

Faulkner registered with a shipping office for passage to Europe as soon as it was available. He expected to be able while waiting for a boat to live in the Quarter on one dollar a day and hoped to earn the money by writing. As soon as he finished the first of his short sketches of New Orleans life, which he at once regarded as part of a series, he took it to the *Times-Picayune*. It was well received, and he was asked to submit additional sketches. By the end of January he had sold the newspaper five sketches and had received a total of twenty dollars, which pleased him and encouraged him to hope that after he went abroad he could earn perhaps ten dollars a week by mailing European sketches back to the paper.

Before his first five accepted sketches had begun to appear in the *Times-Picayune*, Faulkner had sold the newspaper another ten dollars' worth. He had also been able to sell "New Orleans" to *The Double Dealer* in early February for a small fee, which he viewed as a remarkable achievement because he was told, though inaccurately, that the magazine had always received so many contributions from people eager to see their works published free that it had paid no other contributor except Sherwood Anderson.

In early February Faulkner said that he had been postponing his departure for Europe because he had been enjoying his new life in New Orleans but that he had decided to leave in a few weeks if he could get passage. It is possible that he had been waiting until after Sherwood Anderson would return from his combined lecturing and writing tour. That Anderson was interested in Faulk-

ner is clear from his "A Meeting South." And Faulkner
—as he pointed out that spring in the essay reprinted as an
appendix of this volume—was impressed by Anderson's
indigenous quality, his being an "American, and more
than that, a middle westerner, of the soil."

Faulkner possibly had another reason for deciding at
this time to stay on at least a little longer in New Orleans:
he had just begun formal planning of his first novel,
Soldiers' Pay, which, contrary to subsequent reports, he
had not brought to New Orleans as a half-finished manuscript. He may have wanted to get its writing well started
before leaving the city.

In early March, after a farewell visit to his family,
Faulkner returned to New Orleans, expecting to stay less
than a week at the apartment of William Spratling before
taking a boat to Europe. But he again postponed sailing
and moved into a small apartment which he was to rent
for four months until he embarked in July, bound for
Italy. The apartment was on the ground floor at Number
624 Orleans Alley, the picturesque little street, now called
Pirates Alley for the tourist trade, which runs beside the
pleasant ground of St. Anthony's Garden at the rear of
St. Louis Cathedral.

In that Orleans Alley apartment Faulkner settled down
to steady work on his first novel. It became customary
for his neighbors in the building, they later recalled, to
hear his typewriter running full blast from very early
morning. But as he worked on the book which was to
inaugurate his career as a novelist, he retained his con-
ception of himself as a poet. He asked one critic in an
eager letter to give him hard-headed, frank criticism of
his poems. And with irritation he rejected loose praise of

them: When a Mississippian sent him a letter complimenting his "true poetic lines" in *The Marble Faun*, Faulkner derided this unusable response and sent to Oxford for Phil Stone's amusement a copy of his seemingly courteous but actually ironic reply to this insufficiently analytical fan.

Sherwood Anderson and Faulkner began to be together often, sauntering in the Quarter and along the Mississippi River docks, and sitting at cafés and in Jackson Square. In addition to the week-end trip together on a riverboat which Faulkner mentions in his Dallas newspaper essay, they joined in at least one boating excursion on Lake Pontchartrain which was to contribute to Faulkner's novel *Mosquitoes*, where Anderson would appear in part as the character named Dawson Fairchild.

Both men later reported that their association had turned Faulkner toward fiction, and that Anderson had been influential in placing Faulkner's first novel with Anderson's new publisher, Horace Liveright. Some years later Faulkner dedicated his third published novel, *Sartoris*, "TO SHERWOOD ANDERSON *through whose kindness I was first published, with the belief that this book will give him no reason to regret that fact.*"

The relationship between the two men later cooled and Anderson probably resented Faulkner's parody of him in 1926 in the introduction to *Sherwood Anderson & Other Famous Creoles*, as he did the harsher parody of him by Hemingway in *Torrents of Spring*. But in spite of his irritation, Anderson throughout his life showed no signs at all of regretting his early sponsorship of Faulkner's writing: He told Liveright that Faulkner had a good future; he wrote Maxwell Perkins that stories by Hemingway and Faulkner gave him "a grand thrill"; he told his friend Roger Sergel that Faulkner and Hemingway had not "sold out their imaginative life"; he wrote in 1935 that "Stark Young and his sort ignore" the "beaten, ignorant, Bible-ridden, white South" of Huey Long but that "Faulkner occasionally really touches it"; in the same year he listed Faulkner and Hemingway among the professional writers who properly knew themselves to be "real" writers; and in 1937 he wrote that Faulkner, like Thomas Wolfe, "may write of terrible happenings, but you feel always an inner sympathy with the facts of life itself."

Faulkner later said that what he called "the unhappy caricature affair" of *Sherwood Anderson & Other Famous Creoles* led Anderson to decline to see him for years. They apparently met only a few more times: at a cocktail party in New York, when Faulkner realized once again that Anderson was "a giant in an earth populated to a great—too great—extent by pygmies," and at a writers' conference held by the University of Virginia during 1931, when they must have had little communication in the large crowd, where the other celebrities ranged from Ellen Glasgow, James Branch Cabell, and John Peale Bishop to the author of the then popular *Mrs. Wiggs of the Cabbage Patch.* Later they met in New York a time or two. In 1940, not long before he died, Anderson wrote for the Gotham Book Mart's *We Moderns* a brief account of his association with Faulkner in New Orleans, and praised more than his fiction, saying that Faulkner was a "story teller but he was something else too. The man is what they mean in the South when they use the word 'gentle.' He is always that. Life may be at times infinitely vulgar. Bill never is."

Sherwood Anderson & Other Famous Creoles, with its skillful parody by Faulkner of Anderson's style, was the product of a collaboration between Faulkner and the artist William Spratling, whom Faulkner mentions occasionally in the *Times-Picayune* sketches which are being reprinted here. Spratling, who later moved to Taxco, was then a teacher in the Tulane University school of architecture. He lived on an upper floor of the building in Orleans Alley in which Faulkner rented the ground floor. In the *Times-Picayune* sketch entitled "Out of Nazareth," Faulkner names Spratling as his companion on a walk in the Quarter and refers to him as one "whose hand has been shaped to a brush as mine has (alas!) not." Faulkner, long interested in drawing and painting, had shown skill in making drawings for his unpublished play *Marionettes* and for the annual and a humor magazine at the University of Mississippi, and a good sense of color in the paintings which illustrate his unpublished *Mayday.* But he no longer had serious aspirations to be a professional graphic artist: in "Out of Nazareth" he wrote not only that Spratling's hand was "shaped to a brush," but that for himself "words are my meat and bread and drink." To pool these talents, Spratling and Faulkner collaborated in 1926 on *Sherwood Anderson & Other Famous Creoles.* The previous year Miguel Covarrubias had published *The Prince of Wales and Other Famous Americans,* a book of caricatures of American celebrities. In frank imitation of and *"With Respectful Deference to* MIGUEL COVARRUBIAS," Spratling drew for *Sherwood Anderson & Other Famous Creoles* cartoon portraits of forty-one members of the artistic and literary circles of New Orleans, beginning with Sherwood Anderson and including Roark Bradford, then an editor of the *Times-Picayune;* John McClure; Lillian Friend Marcus, sketched as though for an illustration on the cover of *The Double Dealer;* W. C. Odiorne, the photographer, who had recently left New Orleans for Paris and is pictured at the Dome; Caroline Durieux, the artist; Hamilton Basso, then studying at Tulane; and Lyle Saxon. The book ended with a caricature of Spratling and Faulkner, well supplied by three jugs, drawing and writing under a wall sign proclaiming "Viva Art." They dedicated the volume "TO ALL THE ARTFUL AND CRAFTY ONES OF THE FRENCH QUARTER." Spratling recalled that they "unloaded 400 copies on friends at $1.50."

One of the most colorful among the friends who probably bought this book was a man who intrigued Faulkner in those New Orleans months: Colonel Charles Glenn Collins. He was a Scot whose conversational skill and candor made days in the boats and on the beaches of Lake Pontchartrain pleasant for Faulkner and his friends. His had been a life of adventurous ups and downs, as his manuscript autobiography, kindly lent me by his family, clearly shows. Its most noteworthy feature as far as New Orleans was concerned had ended not long before Faulkner reached the city: because of the Colonel's alleged failure to pay for $50,000 worth of jewelry in Bombay, he was held for a time in jail at New Orleans while he made what the New Orleans *Item* reported to be the longest fight against extradition in American history. According to local rumor his incarceration had one charming feature: his jailers regarded him so highly that he could charter a yacht from time to time and cruise about Lake Pontchartrain entertaining the jailers and his literary and artistic friends. Early in 1924 he was completely freed of the charges and returned to life in the Quarter. The Colonel was in part the model for a character in Faulkner's novel *Mosquitoes*—as were several other members of Faulkner's New Orleans group.

It is possible that a few suggestions for the character in *Mosquitoes* named Pete, or for his older brother, Joe, and more suggestions for a character in the *Times-Picayune* sketch "Country Mice," came from the life of a man called "Slim," a vital adjunct of the Quarter's artistic circles during Prohibition. As the New Orleans *Item* recalled at the time of "Slim's" murder in 1937, "His association with liquor establishments in the Vieux Carre made him one of the best known men in that section, it was said." He was a man who commanded attention—and William Faulkner's interest. One former reporter for the *Times-Picayune* remembers that some of the young men on the staff banked their money with "Slim," who would dole it out to them in small, regular amounts to help budget their expenditures, for no one would have thought of arguing with him. He was well read, ran his business affairs smoothly, and kept out of the papers during his active professional career. He is said to have used many boats in his business; and just possibly it was with him that Faulkner, in an episode he later described, went across the Lake into the Gulf to lie-to without lights until the Coast Guard patrols had passed.

The writer Roark Bradford, one year older than Faulkner, was another of his New Orleans acquaintances.

Bradford admired him as a man and as an artist. A few years later, when Faulkner had published novels, Bradford told New Orleans friends that he considered him the greatest writer in America. They spent many leisure hours together, often shared with their mutual friend John McClure. One of their favorite spots was a table in the corner of a cabaret in Franklin Street just off Canal, where the playing of the talented jazz clarinetist George ("Georgia Boy") Boyd especially delighted Faulkner. Another café where these friends spent some of their time was one which the owner is said to have used as his business headquarters in directing much of the section's prostitution but which he ran with notable decorum— and considerable style, serving the best Roquefort sandwiches John McClure remembered ever having tasted. On those occasions Faulkner is reported to have let the others do most of the talking—as he did when he was with these same friends and others at the *Times-Picayune* offices, according to one of the former reporters, Mr. George Tichenor, who has recalled that the younger men "looked up to stars of real magnitude on the city staff. There were at the time Roark Bradford, John McClure, Lyle Saxon, Gwen Bristow, a little Englishman named Eddie Dix, who turned out to be a lord incognito, and several assorted crackpots of dash and ability. Dorothy Dix was retired but chummy."

The *Times-Picayune*'s Sunday magazine published the first of Faulkner's sketches on February 8, 1925. People have said that Sherwood Anderson stimulated Faulkner to write fiction, and Faulkner himself generously supported that view; but the earliest among these sketches and stories in the *Times-Picayune*, as well as the short prose pieces of "New Orleans" which appeared in the earliest issue of *The Double Dealer* for 1925, were certainly not the product of Sherwood Anderson's daily example as a writer, because, as has been noted above, Anderson was not then in New Orleans. But whatever their inspiration, these apprentice sketches and stories, written in part out of Faulkner's need for the newspaper's small payments, foreshadowed some of his mature subsequent work. As the series progressed, Faulkner moved closer to his later subjects, finally even taking up one element of his characteristic subject matter by setting "The Liar" in the back country, far removed from New Orleans, the French Quarter, and Chartres Street.

In selecting "Mirrors of Chartres Street" as the title for his first sketch and as the subtitle for many of his other *Times-Picayune* pieces, Faulkner was being ironical. The *Times-Picayune* carried a "Mirrors of Washington" column full of accounts of people in national affairs; and Harold Begbie's *Mirrors of Downing Street* was extremely popular, with its descriptions of people in London's highest echelons. Faulkner's "Mirrors," held up in a main thoroughfare of the French Quarter, reflect people of a quite different order: The protagonist of the first sketch is a crippled beggar, and the central characters as the series continues include a dynamiter, race-track touts, a pathologically jealous restaurant owner, a jockey, bootleggers, an aged cobbler, and a youthful hoodlum. Instead of being people of substance and power, many of the characters in Faulkner's "Mirrors" are alien, either to American life, like the narrator in "The Cobbler," or to city life, like the confused and victimized up-country Negro in "Sunset." The author shows his respect and sympathy for them, in the first sketch of the series praising the "untrammelled spirit" of the crippled beggar and likening him to "Caesar mounting his chariot among cast roses." Faulkner perceives their hunger—for recognition, for love, for dignity—and makes it a major theme of these sketches.

Just as Faulkner almost immediately expanded some of his short *Double Dealer* pieces into the longer sketches for the *Times-Picayune,* among them "The Cobbler" and "Frankie and Johnny," so he was later to enlarge and enrich in great novels many of his themes from these *Times-Picayune* sketches. The reference in "Out of Nazareth" to the calm belief of a pregnant woman that nature will care for her anticipates Lena Grove of seven years later in *Light in August;* the same sketch, with its comment that the men in the park "had learned that living is not only not passionate or joyous, but is not even especially sorrowful," points in a small way to the attitude Mr. Compson would express to his son Quentin in *The Sound and the Fury.* In "The Kingdom of God" the cornflower blue eyes of the idiot, his broken narcissus, his bellowing, and his silent departure from the final furious scene anticipate the extended and effective treatment of Benjy in *The Sound and the Fury.* The horse which runs through Mrs. Harmon's house in "The Liar" is to grow into the horse which invades Mrs. Littlejohn's house in *The Hamlet,* in fact into the whole wild herd of spotted horses; in the same sketch the store, which would have to be changed only by the addition of the monstrous Flem Snopes to become Will Varner's place at Frenchman's Bend, also anticipates *The Hamlet.* "Yo Ho and Two

Bottles of Rum" points ahead to one of the more startling aspects of *As I Lay Dying*, as the corpse of the too-long dead cabin boy is carted under the blazing sun.

Large motifs are foreshadowed here also. In several of his novels Faulkner was to create, for secular purposes, parallels with Christian belief and ritual, notably in *Sartoris, The Sound and the Fury, As I Lay Dying, Light in August, Pylon, The Hamlet*, and *A Fable*. One of these early sketches shows him making a small beginning of that characteristic practice: "Out of Nazareth" directs the reader by somewhat more than its title to consider a parallel with Christ: Its central character is a youth, innocent and loving, and friendly to the humble of the earth, who has slept in hay among cattle, who is "eternal." Having "served his appointed end" so that he "now need only wait," he is staring at the spire—the cross?—of the cathedral "or perhaps it was something in the sky he was watching." He is on the point of departure, leaving behind him a message of good cheer. He is called David, who has been pointed out by the New Testament and by official religious publications to have been "both a prophet and a type of Jesus Christ." Today to readers aware of Faulkner's later, fully developed practice, the characteristics and experiences of the David in "Out of Nazareth" thinly and in a secular way suggest Christ's, a possibility increased by the fact that this sketch was published in the Easter Sunday issue of the *Times-Picayune* and was not subtitled as part of the "Mirrors of Chartres Street" series despite its setting in the Quarter.

Another motif associated with a religious figure which Faulkner was to expand beyond its appearance in the *Times-Picayune* concerns Saint Francis of Assisi. The sketch, "The Kid Learns," ends when the young gang-ster confronts a girl, "all shining" and with "hair that wasn't brown and wasn't gold and her eyes the color of sleep," and learns as he dies that she is Little Sister Death. This use of Sister Death, whom Saint Francis on his deathbed added to his famous "Canticle of Creatures," was to reappear in Faulkner's work. In a general way it seems already to have been in his poem "The Lilacs," published by *The Double Dealer* in June, 1925, but writ-ten much earlier. More significant use of it is in a later, unpublished work closely associated with *The Sound and the Fury* and titled *Mayday*. When the protagonist of *Mayday*, Sir Galwyn of Arthgyl, has rid himself of Hunger, a companion who has been on his right hand, and of Pain, a companion who has been on his left hand, and is approaching his death by drowning in a river, he gladly joins a maiden shining in the water, who, he learns from Saint Francis, is Little Sister Death. A published later use of this motif, more elaborate because of prob-lems about the protagonist's actual sister, was to be in *The Sound and the Fury* when Quentin Compson, that novel's central monologist, also ridding himself of a kind of hunger embodied in his brother Benjy, the monologist who faces us from Quentin's right hand, and of a kind of pain embodied in his brother Jason, the monologist who faces us from Quentin's left hand, broods on Saint Francis who had "said Little Sister Death" and goes to his own death by drowning in a river.

Elements of Faulkner's later techniques are in these early pieces, which also show at times his mature power, control, and confidence, even though the series is very often marred by his groping, in apprenticeship, for style and literary attitude. For example, his inexperienced handling of the internal monologue of "Home" in no way would lead the reader to anticipate that only four years later William Faulkner would write in *The Sound and the Fury* some of the best interior monologue ever published.

During the period when he was contributing most of these sketches to the *Times-Picayune*, Faulkner was hard at work on his first novel, *Soldiers' Pay*. According to friends he originally gave it the title *Mayday*, which he later used instead as the title of the unpublished allegorical work just mentioned above. According to both Faulkner and Sherwood Anderson, Anderson brought the manuscript of *Soldiers' Pay* to the attention of Horace Liveright, who had just become Anderson's publisher. Liveright's house was then at the height of its success and was to bring out during the next twelve months not only Faulkner's first novel and Hemingway's *In Our Time*, but also Anderson's *Dark Laughter*, Robinson Jeffers' *Roan Stallion*, Dreiser's *American Tragedy*, Roger Martin du Gard's *The Thibaults*, and editions of T. S. Eliot, Ezra Pound, O'Neill, and Freud.

But Liveright's firm did not reach its decision to publish *Soldiers' Pay* until late August, 1925; and by then Faulkner was no longer in New Orleans, having at last left on his repeatedly postponed first trip to Europe. When he and Spratling sailed from the Port of New Orleans on July 7, 1925, as passengers aboard the freighter *West Ivis*, the *Times-Picayune* had already published twelve of his signed sketches. He may have written and left with the editors one more sketch, "The Liar," and perhaps a second, "Episode." "The Liar" appeared in the issue for July 26, while Faulkner was at sea, but he may have written it aboard the *West Ivis* and mailed it to the *Times-Picayune* from Savannah, where the ship lay from July 11 through July 14 to discharge cargo and take aboard rosin and linters for its run to Naples. This seems a good possibility, for though the *Times-Picayune* had published a sketch by Faulkner in every Sunday issue during April and May, it had published none in June or in July before the twenty-sixth, and former members of the staff doubt very much that the rather hastily put together Sunday magazine section of those days would have held such a sketch in reserve. "The Liar" is Faulkner's first published story with the rural setting he was to use so successfully in some of his greatest fiction. And one may speculate on the possibility that once at sea he broke his series about the New Orleans French Quarter to produce this story which foreshadowed so much of his later work.

By the time "Episode" appeared in the *Times-Picayune*, Faulkner and Spratling had disembarked at Genoa, August 2; and Faulkner was beginning to rove over much of northern Italy, visiting Stresa; Piacenza; Pavia, where the quiet of the city and the peace at the inn, Pesce d'Oro, delighted him; and a small village in the mountains where he lived during part of August with farmers, sharing their work and leisure and writing an unpublished travelogue.

In September, when "Country Mice" appeared in the *Times-Picayune*, Faulkner, after traveling through Switzerland, had been living in Paris for some time, at 26 Rue Servandoni. As in New Orleans, he was only a few steps from the open space surrounding a church—Saint Sulpice

—and he was even nearer the freedom of a park more spacious than Jackson Square—the Luxembourg Gardens, where he spent much of his time.

For hours he helped children sail their toy boats on the Luxembourg's great pool, especially noting an old man with battered hat and enraptured expression who played with the toy boats too—and was to reappear years later in the final scene of *Sanctuary*, when children and a shabbily dressed old man are sailing boats in the Luxembourg Gardens as Temple Drake sits yawning there beside her father in the avenue of statues of great queens. But Faulkner, by no means suffering the boredom of Miss Drake, was writing. While the *Times-Picayune* was printing the last of these sketches, "Yo Ho and Two Bottles of Rum," with its ocean voyage for which he may have drawn in small part on his trip to Genoa aboard the *West Ivis*, Faulkner was at work in the Luxembourg Gardens on a novel, and had just completed a short story. Years later when asked whether it was his practice to write by a schedule or when the spirit moved him, he replied that it was only when the spirit moved him, but it moved him every day.

He returned from France to New York at the end of 1925 and reached Mississippi in time for the Christmas holidays with his family. The next autumn he gave the following account of the winter, spring, and summer of 1926 to a New Orleans reporter:

> William Faulkner, native of Oxford, Mississippi, who wrote "Soldiers' Pay" . . . returned to the Vieux Carre Sunday to plan a winter's work. Incidentally, he announced the publication of "Mosquitoes," another novel.

Introduction

. . . Mr. Faulkner, sun-tanned from working as a fisherman on a Pascagoula schooner, and sucking an inscribed pipe, won last Spring when he shot a hole in one while acting as a professional at the Oxford golf club, sat in an apartment in the old town and watched the rain-splashed roofs . . .

He told of a summer spent working in a lumber mill, until a finger was injured, and then on the fishing boats of the Mississippi coast. At nights, after working hours, he wrote his new book.

Monday, he will return to Oxford for a short stay and at the end of September he will return to this city for the winter.

Faulkner was still writing poetry—as he had done in New Orleans and had continued to do on his trip to Europe. A number of unpublished sonnets which survive from that period he dated from New Orleans and the Mississippi gulf coast, at sea on the *West Ivis* and off Majorca and Minorca, and from Italy and Paris. For eight more years he occasionally published poems in periodicals; and *A Green Bough*, greatly revised from its original manuscript form, appeared in 1933. But in 1925 at New Orleans he had turned to fiction with full force. During the following years, by developing many of his themes, techniques, thoughts, and feelings which first appeared, often dimly, in these apprentice pieces, William Faulkner published more than twenty volumes of fiction, some of them among the best to appear so far in our century.

CARVEL COLLINS

New Orleans Sketches

New Orleans

———◆———

Wealthy Jew

"**I** LOVE THREE THINGS: gold; marble and purple; splendor, solidity, color." The waves of Destiny, foaming out of the East where was cradled the infancy of the race of man, roaring over the face of the world. Let them roar: my race has ridden them. Upon the tides of history has my * race ever put forth, bravely, mayhap foolhardily, as my ancient Phoenician ancestors breasted the uncharted fabulous seas with trading barques, seeking those things which I, too, love. Suns rise and set; ages of man rise and joy and battle and weep, and pass away. Let them: I, too, am but a lump of moist dirt before the face of God. But I am old, all the pain and passion and sorrows of the human race are in this breast: joys to fire, griefs to burn out the soul.

* In the original text this word is "may." Similar obvious typographical errors in the sketches from both *The Double Dealer* and the *Times-Picayune* have been corrected without notation. When there has been any doubt, the original form has been retained and noted.

But from these bitter ashes which are I, heirs to my pleasures and pains will rise phoenix-like, for the blood is old, but strong. O ye mixed races, with your blood mingled and thinned and lost; with your dream grown tarnished and pointless, knowing not what ye desire! My people offered you a dream of peace that passeth understanding, and arid Syrian sands drank the blood of your young men; I flung you a golden coin, and you purchased martyrdom of Death in Ahenobarbus' gardens; ye took Destiny from the hands of my people, and your sons and my sons lay together in the mud at Passchendaele and sleep side by side beneath foreign soil. Foreign? What soil is foreign to me? Your Alexanders and Caesars and Napoleons rise in blood and gold, shrieking briefly of home, and then are gone as waves hiss curling on the beach, and die. No soil is foreign to my people, for have we not conquered all lands with the story of your Nativity? The seas of Destiny foam by. Let them! My people will crest them, mayhap to be swept like blown trumpets among the cold stars.

"I love three things: gold; marble and purple; splendor, solidity, color."

The Priest

EVENING LIKE A NUN shod with silence, evening like a girl slipping along the wall to meet her lover. . . . The twilight is like the breath of contented kine, stirring among the lilacs and shaking spikes of bloom, ringing the soundless bells of hyacinths dreaming briefly of Lesbos, whispering among the pale and fronded palms.

Ah, God, ah, God. The moon is a silver sickle about to mow the rose of evening from the western sky; the moon is a little silver boat on green and shoreless seas. Ave, Maria, deam. . . . How like birds with golden wings the measured bell notes fly outward and upward, passing with clear and faint regret the ultimate slender rush of cross and spire; and how like the plummet lark the echo, singing, falls. Ave, Maria. . . . Ah God, ah God, that night should come so soon.

Orion through the starry meadows strays, the creaking Wain breaks darkly through the Milky Way's faint dewed grass. Sorrow, and love that passeth away. Ave, Maria! a little silver virgin, hurt and sad and pitiful, re-membering Jesus' mouth upon her breast. Mortification, and the flesh like a babe crying among dark trees . . . "hold my hair fast, and kiss me through it—so: Ah, God, ah God, that day should be so soon!"

Ave, Maria; deam gratiam . . . tower of ivory, rose of Lebanon . . .

Frankie and Johnny

LISTEN, BABY, before I seen you it was like I was one of them ferry boats yonder, crossing and crossing a dark river or something by myself; acrossing and acrossing and never getting nowheres and not knowing it and thinking I was all the time. You know—being full of a lot of names of people and things busy with their own business, and thinking I was the berries all the time. And say, listen:

When I seen you coming down the street back yonder

it was like them two ferry boats hadn't seen each other until then, and they would stop when they met instead of crossing each other, and they would turn and go off side by side together where they wasn't nobody except them. Listen, baby: before I seen you I was just a young tough like what old Ryan, the cop, says I was, not doing nothing and not worth nothing and not caring for nothing except old Johnny. But when that drunk bum stopped you and said what he said to you and I walked up and slammed him, I done it for you and not for me; and it was like a wind had blew a lot of trash and stuff out of the street.

And when I put my arm around you and you was holding to me and crying, I knowed you was meant for me even if I hadn't never seen you before, and that I wasn't no longer the young tough like what old Ryan, the cop, says I was; and when you kissed me it was like one morning a gang of us was beating our way back to town on a rattler and the bulls jumped us and trun us off and we walked in and I seen day breaking acrost the water when it was kind of blue and dark at the same time, and the boats was still on the water and there was black trees acrost, and the sky was kind of yellow and gold and blue. And a wind come over the water, making funny little sucking noises. It was like when you are in a dark room or something, and all on a sudden somebody turns up the light, and that's all. When I seen your yellow hair and your gray eyes it was like that: It was like a wind had blew clean through me and there was birds singing somewheres. And then I knowed it was all up with me.

Oh, Johnny!

Baby!

The Sailor

AH, TO HAVE PAVEMENT under my feet again, instead
of a motionless becalmed deck—motionless as a rock
thrust up from the sea's bottom, with the very pitch
starting from the seams and shrouds and canvas heavy
and dead in a breathless noon. Or plunging and tacking
off the bitter Horn! Icy and stiffened the gear, and cold-
blisters like boils on every man's hands. But here is a
stationary world: she don't pitch and groan and boom,
not she! nor, scuppers under, race the howling gale.

Ah, lads, only fools go to sea—unless it be for to change
women occasionally. Surely a man cannot be satisfied with
one kind for ever. There's your wide-hipped Spaniard
among the mandolins in the smoky inn, your blonde
Norse women, your pale cold Anglo-Saxons. And I mind
one I met beneath the walls of Yemen; red haired, she
was; and one in the Chinee ocean: knifed three men. And
where's a man to make his final port, with all these from
which to choose?

A sound footing is good, and wine and women and
fighting; but soon the fighting's done and the wine is
drunk and women's mouths dont taste as sweet as a man
had thought, and then he'll sicken for the surge and the
sound of the sea, and the salt smell of it again.

The Cobbler

MY LIFE IS A HOUSE: the smell of leather is the wall
of my house. Three sides are dark, but from the other

side there comes faint light through dingy unwashed windows. Beyond these windows the world grows loud and passes away. I was once a part of the world, I was once a part of the rushing river of mankind; but now I am old, I have been swirled into a still backwater in a foreign land, and the river has left me behind. That river of which I was once a part, I do not remember very well, for I am old: I have forgotten much.

Joy and sorrow—what mean these? Did I know once? But joy and sorrow are the birds which whirl screaming above the rushing flood: they do not bother about backwaters. Peace I know in setting properly a nail, in fixing cunningly a sole, and in my wife. My wife? This bush of golden roses is my wife. See, how the ancient branches are twisted and gnarled with age, as this hand is twisted and gnarled and old. Yet each year it bears me sweet bloom, though it be as old in years as I.

Ah, Tuscany! and the belled flocks among the sunny hills long after the valley itself was in shadow! and feast days and dancing on the green, and she in her scarlet kerchief, her cloudy tossing hair and her sweet wild breasts arbored amid her hair! But we were promised, you see.

She and this rose and I were young together, she and I, who were promised, and a flung rose in the dust, under the evening star. But now that rose is old in a pot, and I am old and walled about with the smell of leather, and she—and she . . . I have known joy and sorrows, but now I do not remember. I am old: I have forgotten much.

The Longshoreman

"SHE WOULDN'T do what I asked her to, so I socked her in the jaw . . ." Jesus, look down: see dat barrel ro-o-o-ll! White folks says, and nigger does. Load dat steamboat, load her down; O steamboat, spread white wings and fly! Streaks of sunlight cutting the wall's shadow, slide up me, barring my overalls and my black hands with stripes of gold, like a jail suit. Sinners in jail, sinners in heaven, behind dem bars of gold! I got wings, you got wings, all God's chillen got wi-i-n-gs. . . . But, ah God, the light on the river, and the sun; and the night, the black night, in this heart. Oh, the black night, and the thudding drums sultry among the stars. The stars are cold, O God, and the great trees sailing like ships up the rivers of darkness, brushing the ancient stars forever aside, in vain. The earth alone is warm, heated by the dead buried in it. But the dead are cold, O lord, in the warm and the dark. Sweet chariot, comin' fer t' cyah me home; sweet chariot! wash me whiter'n sno-o-w!

Quittin' time, whistles boomin' and moanin' like front row sinners at meetin' time. Ah God, the singing blood, the sultry blood, singing to the fierce fire in the veins of girls, singing the ancient embers into flame! White man gives me clo'se and shoes, but dat dont make no pavement love my feets. These cities are not my cities, but this dark is my dark, with all the old passions and fears and sorrows that my people have breathed into it. Let this blood sing: did I make this blood?

I got wings, you got wings; all God's chillen got w-i-i-n-g-s-s!

The Cop

WHEN I WAS YOUNG, running about like a puppy or a colt, doing all the things which seemed to me grander than kings or even policemen could do (things which somebody always thought I oughtn't to do) and being heartily wished dead by half the neighborhood in consequence, there was but one person in the world with whom I would have exchanged. Fellows there were who intended to be pirates, some would go west and kill Indians gallantly from loping horses, others would sit in the cabs of locomotives, blowing derisive whistle blasts at lesser adventurous mortals. But I, I would be a patrolman; in a blue coat and swinging a casual stick and with a silver shield on my breast, I would space the streets away with the measured beat of my footsteps.

What to compare with this grandeur? To be the idol and fear of the lads, to be looked upon with respect by even grown people; to be the personification of bravery and the despair of criminals; to have a real pistol in my pocket! Later, in my adolescent years, this glamorous figure still paraded solemnly, filling my mind. I could see myself, huge and calm, negligently talking with admiring girls, being fed cake and pies and cups of coffee in snug kitchens, treading the lonely streets at night before dark houses where multitudes in slumber turn and sigh and safely dream, for I was there to guard them.

Or, foiling the murderer, shooting him dead in the spitting darkness, and sorely wounded, to be nursed to health again by a beautiful girl, whom I would marry.

But now that lad is grown up. Sometimes I think he

still lurks somewhere within me, reproaching me because the man has been unable to give to the lad that high desire which life has promised him. But he sleeps easily; he does not trouble me often—and what would you? life is not like that. Sometimes, pacing the dark and empty streets, he wakes and I am briefly troubled over the futile bargain a man makes when he exchanges a small body and a great heart for a large body and hardly any heart at all; but not for long. Certainly man does not ever get exactly what he wants in this world, and who can say that a wife and a home and a position in the world are not, after all, the end of every man's desire. Anyway, I prefer to believe that this creature fronting the world bravely in a blue coat and a silver shield is quite a fellow, after all.

The Beggar

WHEN I WAS A BOY I believed passionately that life was more than just eating and sleeping, than restricting a man's life to one tiny speck of the earth's surface and marking his golden hours away to the stroke of a bell. What little of the world the ant can see is good to him; and I, with his vision magnified an hundred times—what would it not be to the ant with my vision! Then multiply the limit of my sight by the size of the earth—and there you are.

Ah, to have mounted heart and sight and sense on such a sorry nag! The knight still would ride forth, but his steed is old and not sure of foot any more; other warriors on younger and lustier stallions override and unhorse him, and now he must whine and snarl with others whose steeds have failed, over gnawed crusts without the relentless gates, in the dusty road.

The Artist

A DREAM AND A FIRE which I cannot control, driving me without those comfortable smooth paths of solidity and sleep which nature has decreed for man. A fire which I inherited willy-nilly, and which I must needs feed with talk and youth and the very vessel which bears the fire: the serpent which consumes its own kind, knowing that I can never give to the world that which is crying in me to be freed.

For where is that flesh, what hand holds that blood to shape this dream within me in marble or sound, on canvas or paper, and live? I, too, am but a shapeless lump of moist earth risen from pain, to laugh and strive and weep, knowing no peace until the moisture has gone out of it, and it is once more of the original and eternal dust.

But to create! Which among ye who have not this fire, can know this joy, let it be ever so fleet?

Magdalen

GOD, THE LIGHT in my eyes, the sunlight flashing through the window, crashing in my poor head like last night's piano. Why didn't I close them damn shutters?

I can remember when I found days gold, but now the gold of day hurts my head. 'Tis night only is gold now, and that not often. Men aint what they used to be, or money aint, or something. Or maybe its I that aint like I was once. God knows, I try to treat 'em like they'd want I should. I treat 'em white as any, and whiter than some—not calling no names. I'm an American girl with an American smile I am, and they know it.

There was wild blood in my veins; when I was young the blood sang like shrill horns through me. I saw women who had the bright things I wanted—dresses and shoes and golden rings, lifting no finger to get them. And lights and sultry music, and all the bright chimaerae of the brain! And ah! my body like music, my body like flame crying for silken sheens a million worms had died to make, and that my body has died a hundred times to wear them. Yes, a thousand worms made this silk, and died; I have died a thousand deaths to wear it; and sometime a thousand worms, feeding upon this body which has betrayed me, feeding, will live.

Was there love once? I have forgotten her. Was there grief once? Yes, long ago. Ah, long ago.

The Tourist

—NEW ORLEANS.

A courtesan, not old and yet no longer young, who shuns the sunlight that the illusion of her former glory be preserved. The mirrors in her house are dim and the frames are tarnished; all her house is dim and beautiful with age. She reclines gracefully upon a dull brocaded chaise-longue, there is the scent of incense about her, and her draperies are arranged in formal folds. She lives in an atmosphere of a bygone and more gracious age.

And those whom she receives are few in number, and they come to her through an eternal twilight. She does not talk much herself, yet she seems to dominate the conversation, which is low-toned but never dull, artificial but not brilliant. And those who are not of the elect must stand forever without her portals.

New Orleans . . . a courtesan whose hold is strong upon the mature, to whose charm the young must respond. And all who leave her, seeking the virgin's un-brown, ungold hair and her blanched and icy breast where no lover has died, return to her when she smiles across her languid fan. . . .

New Orleans.

Mirrors of
Chartres Street

His voice had the hoarseness of vocal cords long dried with alcohol, and he was crippled. I first noticed him when he swung himself across my path with apelike agility and demanded a quarter for bread. His gray thatch and his eyes as wild and soft as a faun's, his neck muscles moving as smooth as an athlete's to the thrust of his crutch, stopped me; his garrulous assurance—"Say, you are a young man now, and you got both legs. But some day you may need a bite of bread and a cup of coffee, just a cup of coffee, to keep the damp out of your bones; and you may stop a gentleman like I'm stopping you, and he may be my son—I was a good one in my day, fellow." I had prided myself at the time on my appearance; that I did not look even like a prospective bum, wearing then tweeds which came from the Strand; but who knows what life may do to us? Anyway, to have such a breath fondly on one's neck in this nation and time was worth a quarter.

Fifteen minutes later I saw him again, handily swinging himself into a movie theater where was one of those million-dollar pictures of dukes and adultery and champagne and lots of girls in mosquito netting and lamp shades. Truly, his was an untrammelled spirit: his the same heaven-sent attribute for finding life good which enabled the Jews to give young Jesus of Nazareth with two stars in His eyes, sucking His mother's breast, and a fairy tale that has conquered the whole Western earth; which gave King Arthur to a dull world; and sent baron and knight and lads who had more than coronets to flap pennons in Syria, seeking a dream.

Later, from a railed balcony—Mendelssohn impervious in iron—I saw him for the last time. The moon had crawled up the sky like a fat spider and planes of light and shadow were despair for the Vorticist schools. (Even those who carved those strange flat-handed creatures on the Temple of Rameses must have dreamed New Orleans by moonlight.)

About the symbolical stolidity of a cop he darted and spun on his crutch like a water beetle about a rock. His voice rose and fell, his crutch-end, arcing in the street lamp, described a rectangle upon the pavement and within this rectangle he became motionless with one movement, like a bird alighting. "This is my room," he proclaimed hoarsely, "now, how can you arrest me, huh? Where's your warrant for entering my room, fellow?"

"I've sent for a warrant," the officer told him. "But I'll get you anyway. You can't stay there all night; you got to leave soon to get a drink."

"I got a drink on me, fellow, and you know it."

"Yeh? Where is it?"

" 'S all right," replied the other, cunningly, "you can't get it without a warrant."

The policeman leaned toward him, pawing at his sorry clothing.

"Take your hands off me," he screamed. He stood miraculously on his single leg and his crutch spun about his head like a propeller blade. "Arrest me in my own room! Arrest me! Where's laws and justice? Ain't I a member of greatest republic on earth? Ain't every laborer got his own home, and ain't this mine? Beat it, you damn Republican. Got a gov'ment job: thinks he can do whatever he wants," he informed the bystanders with hoarse cunning. He swept the crutch back to his armpit, and struck an attitude.

"Listen, men. I was born American citizen and I been a good citizen all my life. When America needs men, who's first to say 'America, take me'? I am, until railroad cut off my leg. And did I do anything to railroad for cutting off my leg? Did I go to railroad president and say, 'Say, do you know you cut off my leg?' No, sir. I said I been good American citizen all my life—all my life I worked hard. I been laboring man, and ain't every laboring man got his own room, and ain't this mine? Now, I ask you, one gentleman to 'nother, can damn Republican come in laboring man's room and arrest him?" He turned again to the cop. "You big coward, come on and arrest me. I got no gun; can't shoot you if I wanted. Come in and arrest me! Come on, now, I dare you. Can't no Republican come in my room without a warrant."

Down the street, clanging among the shivering golden wings of street lights, came the wagon at last. As it stopped at the curb, he hopped nimbly toward it. "Yes, sir," he croaked as he was helped in, "I'm American citizen and laboring man, but when a friend sends car for me, why, I'll go. Yes, sir, never refused a friend in my life, even if he's rich and I ain't nothing but self-respecting American citizen." Half-way in, he turned for recapitulation. "I'm laboring man, own property in town, but I got rich friends. Sam Gompers was my friend; he wouldn't stood by and let damn Republican arrest me, but now poor Sam's dead. Dead and gone, boys, but he was my friend, friend all laboring men."

"Come on, come on," interrupted the officer. "All right, Ed."

He was thrust abruptly in and the wagon clanged away. "So long, cap," he shouted back, the tires sucked over the wet pavement and around the corner; clanging from sight and sound he went, while his voice came hoarsely among the shadows and intermittent light.

"So long, cap."

The policeman turned, his comfortably broad back looked [*sic*] in the light, passed to dark and from shadow to light again; then his heavy footfall faded away.

And one thought of Caesar mounting his chariot among cast roses and the shouts of the rabble, and driving along the Via Appia while beggars crept out to see and centurions clashed their shields in the light of golden pennons flapping across the dawn.

Damon and
Pythias Unlimited

T HE CABILDO, a squat Don who wears his hat in
the king's presence, not for the sake of his own integer
vitae, but because some cannot, gloomed in sinister deri-
sion of an ancient joke; within the portals Iowa wondered aloud first, why a building as old and ugly could
have any value; and second, if it were valuable, why they
let it become so shabby. "I bet the city ain't painted it in
twenty years. Why don't they tear it down, anyway,
and put up a modern building? They would have done
that in Winterset years ago. These people in the South
ain't got the pep we have at all."

I pondered on the mutability of mankind—how imaginative atrophy seems to follow, not the luxuries and vices
of an age as the Baptists teach us, but rather the effi-
ciencies and conveniences such as automatic food and
bathtubs per capita, which should bring about the golden
age. One almost believes that the old farmer, who said he

was not going to dilute his vigor by washing all over every day, was vouchsafed the true light.

A round, very dirty man somehow becomes involved here. I seem to have answered intelligently one or two of his remarks before becoming aware of him. His soft, melting brown eyes—like a spaniel's—bathed me in a moist, hot glow, his broad Semitic face shone, the very hat, once gray and worn rakishly upon his neck, seemed to have the same oily coating. Beyond his olive oil illusion, though, was something that puzzled me for a time. Then I got it: he smacked vaguely of—not horses, exactly, but of stables and racing swipes, and slumber in horse blankets.

"Stranger in town?" I told him yes, and his gaze became hotter upon me. "Noo Orluns nice place, huh?" I agreed to this also, and his gaze became mesmeric as he glibly mispronounced French names; he worked his way to and up Canal street, and then it came. No, I had not been to the races. His stare changed to a fond, protective amazement.

"Ain't seen the races? Why say, mister, to visut Noo Orluns and not see the races is like not eating a meal at Antony's (Antoine's?) cafe. Well, say, you're lucky, you are. I was just on my way out to the races now, and I'll be glad of your company. I know Noo Orluns like a book; I know the racing game as well as any fellow you'll meet. I'll be mighty glad to accommodate a stranger, but I'll be gladder still of your company. I been a chentleman all my life, see; and I know a chentleman when I see one. Morowitz is my name," he ended, taking my arm and removing my hand from my jacket, clasping it heartily in his moist palm.

"Yes, sir, this is your lucky day, all right. I'm sorry I ain't got my car with me. A good friend of mine borrowed it off me this morning, but he'll meet us at the track and I'll be glad to drive you around and show you the city after the races. Come on, we'll get a taxi. I wanta go to my hotel—you at the St. Charles? No? Then we'll go on out."

I was interested in seeing if he really could get in the St. Charles, even in a democracy, but I mentally promised that he should not shake my hand again. A cab passed and he hailed it with arm and voice. The driver slowed down, looked at the two of us, and shouted back:

"Well, whatcher want?"

"None of that, now," my new acquaintance shouted in turn. "Drive over here; my friend and I wanta go to our hotel."

The driver weighed the two of us in his mind, and then he addressed me.

"Are you with him?" I told him that I seemed to be, and he drew up to the curb. My companion leaped for the door, grasping the handle as the driver reached to open the door from within, and for a while the two of them mildly sported with it.

"Come on, come on, fellow. Whata you mean? I'll report you for this."

"Well, turn the goddam handle loose, you —— —— ——."

The door opened at last.

"Drive to the St. Charles, see? My friend and me are in a hurry."

"Well, get in, then. I can't take you or your friend nowheres until you get in the cab."

We sat back, but the driver still regarded us. "Well, where to? You wanta go riding, or to the police station?"

"To the St. Charles, I told you. That's where I always stay when I'm in town."

"Aw, come off, you don't live at the St. Charles."

"Listen, fellow; I'll have you arrested; I'll call a cop."

"You wouldn't no more dare call a cop than you'd dare go to the St. Charles." He looked at me. "Do you want to go to the St. Charles?"

We seemed to have been caught in some horrible vacuum of inactivity, to have no escape. "Do you really live at the St. Charles?" I asked him.

"Well, practically, see? My friend works in the Alhambra Baths right next door to the St. Charles, so what's the good of me staying at a hotel when my friend insists, I stay with him, huh?"

The driver regarded him balefully. "Live at the Alhambra Baths, do you? Ain't been home in a week, though, have you?"

"Huh? Say, listen here, fellow—"

The driver addressed me again. "Take my advice, mister, and throw this bird out and go on where you are going, see?" I had about reached this conclusion myself, but I decided to carry on a bit longer. I asked him to drive us out to the race track, and we were off. Then I found how my companion's hat acquired that peculiar oily sheen. He removed it and mopped his face with it. He became voluble.

"Cheest, it's a shame what a chentleman must stand from these taxi drivers. I tell you, mister, I been a chentleman all my life and I ain't used to depending on taxicabs. But it happened I loaned my car to a friend today.

Tomorrow, though, I'll call for you at your hotel. Listen, I'll put a car at your disposal all day, see? I'm a chentleman and I like a chentleman's company. Yes, sir, tomorrow they won't no friend of mine be insulted again by—" he nodded toward the driver's back and his lowered voice became obscene. I stopped him, revolted; and forbade his speaking again until we reached the track.

He hopped briskly out when the cab stopped, thrusting his fingers in his vest. "Got change for a twenty?" The corner of a bill showed in his fingers—a twenty.

The driver whipped out the meter receipt viciously. "Who you think I am—Carnegie?"

"I'll pay the cab," I interrupted. "You can get your bill changed at the gate."

"No, no," he said hastily, "I got some change—here you are, fellow. And when you drive chentlemen, learn to behave yourself."

The driver's reply was lost in the roar of his engine. "Get two," he continued to me, "I'll hand it back to you inside."

I got two tickets and we passed the turnstiles. A race was just over, and through the pandemonium of the eight-to-ones we shoved our way, and out before the stands. The track flew smoothly past, swooped circling: a long rush and another turn and it swept into the home stretch—a graceful oval grassed with such a green as to seem poisonous; as if man or beast might take one bite and drop, stricken. The merry silks of riders flashed in the paddock and small puffy clouds fought a celestial handicap overhead.

"—said before, I know a chentleman when I see one, and I am proud of your acquaintance. Yes, sir; when I like a man I'm his friend, and I'll take care of him: he won't want for nothing. Now, this little jock I'm telling you about, he's my cousin, see? He's got inside information on every race run here. He's right, or he couldn't fool me—I been in this game too long to be took in. Listen, I followed the races all over the world: I been to 'em in Parrus, and in England I been to 'em; and I vouch for this little jock like he was my own brother, see? Listen, he couldn't fool you if I wasn't here taking care of you— you been around[,] I can see that. When you see him I bet you'll say he got the most intellichent face you ever seen: you watch what I say. But the boy's down on his luck right now. He's overweight a little and he's got a cough, not bad, but just enough so he can't take off this here overweight. So he ain't riding now.

"Now, he's got a jock friend in hospital: got no money, no nothing. I swear I like to cried when he told me about this poor boy laying up there with doctors cutting on him all day long; got no money, no nothing. I got a kind heart, mister, I admit it; and when I like a man I like him, see? Now, what you say we donate five dollars out of every bet we win for this poor boy laying up in hospital? We won't miss it, after the killing we'll make on these tips of this cousin of mine. You and me, all we want is a little sport: we don't need the money; but I always say if you can have your sport and clean up beside, why do it, I always say. Here he is now—hey, jock!"

He approached, a thin lad in an extreme suit. His face had a smooth, faintly girlish oval and his eyes were kind and frank and gray, despite their sophistication. But one look at his flat, spare shoulders and thin chest was enough to know that it was no mere cough he had, poor boy.

There was foreknowledge of certain death in his eyes. My companion, without a trace of humor, introduced his cousin, Mr. McNamara. I took to him at once, and five dollars was quickly agreed on.

Four of his tips ran true to form in succession—just tips. They both guaranteed the last one, though—if the beast stood up he simply could not lose. I here noticed that I was the only one risking any actual money. They were both quick to show me their bets on paper.

"But you still have your twenty-dollar bill," I reminded my first sponsor. "This race is a sure thing, you say. Why not plunge on it and recover?" No, no! This would not do. Even the angle of his hat became voluble. "Let me see your bill," I said. He demurred and tried to change the conversation.

"Let me see your bill," I repeated.

He produced it reluctantly, a twenty-dollar silver certificate issued by the Confederate States of America in 1862. I returned it to him.

Then the last race was run, and sure enough our horse won handily, netting me some two or three dollars after subtracting the promised fiver.

They both offered to deliver it, the boy with insistent politeness; while the other, still vocal, demanded, insisted, cajoled; pawing and rubbing my arms, trying to take the bill from my hand. We were beginning to attract attention.

"Listen, mister, I been a chentleman all my life. You think I would put anything over on another chentleman? Listen, you got me wrong. Listen, you give me that money and I'll—"

"Ah, beat it! Go on, you bum. Say, mister, don't listen

to him. If he gets his hands on that money they won't nobody ever see a cent of it."

The other flung his hands heavenward. "Will you now listen to him! Insulting a chentleman and my friend before my very eyes! How much of that money now do you think he gives away yet? Listen: there ain't a worser one in Noo Orluns than him."

"Shut your mouth," the boy shouted, taking my arm. "Shut your mouth! He don't know you!"

"Don't know me! Who brought him here, huh? Did you? Say, listen, mister—"

"Don't pay him no attention, mister. I admit I ain't going to give this money to no one; I won't try to put nothing over you no longer. If you don't believe me, just keep this five and meet me tomorrow anywhere you say. I'll show you I'm square. Just keep the money and I'll meet you tomorrow and bring you out, and I'll treat you right."

The other screamed in utter anguish. "As God is my witness, he will rob you in spite of me. Listen, mister, say the word and I will call a cop to take up this noosance."

"Call a cop? You don't dare call a cop! Listen, mister—"

"Listen, mister! Don't you have nothing to do with that fellow. You don't know him, see? Listen: you give me your hotel number and I'll call for you in my car tomorrow, and we'll make a killing. It's four hundred ahead today I am, and tomorrow we'll clean up, see?"

"Four hundred ahead? Call for you in his car? Say, mister, did he say what kind of car he's got? Well, it was a Ford two years ago; I dunno what he calls it now. And he can't call for nobody in it because it's in hock for two dollars and a half. That's what he wants that five bucks for."

The other leaped upon him, shrieking. They struggled. Locked in close embrace they swayed about the floor. "You would rob me!" hissed the other, "you will give me nothing!" The lad flung him off. "Ah, I'll get your car out for you. But if you keep on I'll give you a smack in the jaw." The boy took my arm again.

"Listen, sir," he whispered hurriedly, "it ain't your money I want, it's your friendship, see? Meet me at the St. Charles at noon tomorrow with five hundred dollars, and we'll make a killing, sure. Don't fool with that bum no more. Keep the five, and I'll meet you at twelve sharp."

The other surged between us, breathing heavily. "Say, fellow, move off and let me speak to my friend in private, will you?"

The lad shook my hand, gave me a meaning look, and drew back. The other pawed me affectionately, trying to put his arms around my neck. I won, and he was forced to hiss his message from at least a foot's distance: "Listen, mister: I'm your friend, see? I've been a chentleman all my life; I'm accustomed to associating with chentlemen; me and you don't want to fool with no bums, see?" (Meantime the bum was flashing me knowing winks over my present confidant's round and oblivious head.) "You ain't gave him no money, have you? No? Well, listen: I'll call [for] you tomorrow, in my car, and we'll come out and clean up. What's your hotel?"

"Meet me at the St. Charles at twelve sharp," I told him. He released me and I moved away, leaving them glaring at each other across the empty room.

Home

A MAN sat on the curb. In his hands were a carpenter's saw and a violin bow. The saw he held like a violin and from the bow there rose a sound, a resonant singing, half string and half pipe, which the very atmosphere, which silence itself, seemed to find strange and hard to digest: toying with it when the bow ceased—a lilting provencal air played in a virgin tonal scale, and somehow ambiguously martial.

* * *

Jean-Baptiste leaned motionless in a dark areaway, feeling the darkness flow past him down the street, watching the quiet roof-tops cutting the sky, watching the stars like cast roses arrested above an open coffin. He was thinking of the dark corners which men's destinies turn. His decision he could still revoke, though, there was yet time; and this very fact was a part of his unease. To get it over with! To be either flesh or fowl, instead of being neither, of having decided definitely to be the one and then being forced to wait, and think. Thinking, indeed, lays lads underground.

If he could only forget that his decision might still be revoked! How simple things would then be. To decide, to act; and once and for all put himself beyond the pale. But as it was, he could see now how the heat of the moment, his present despairs, had tricked him. But it was not too late! There was still time.

True, there was his broken word. What would Pete and the General and Tony the Wop think of him? What would that thing within himself that knew not hunger nor sleep nor time, say to him? He had passed his word, you couldn't get around that. And he hated the nimbleness of his fingers, his knowledge of explosive, for he believed that had he been an ordinary immigrant living a dull life as an honest, unimaginative artisan, he would have escaped this temptation and the need of making this decision.

But it went further back than that. He thought of his boyhood in the South; of a thatched cottage near a forest where he roamed in the spring, of the airs of May within the chestnut trees. Remembering it in this kindhearted, impossible America was like remembering a song: through the twilight his waiting bowl of supper called him; there in the soft candle light he ate, and slept the night away on his pallet while the day of sun cooled [in?] his quick blood. Of his wild and joyous adolescence he thought, and of his canny peasant mother, whose despair his young years had been, saying: "How this war is terrible! and how it has made a man of that Jean-Baptiste!"

A man, indeed! He thought of his platoon tramping newly through the mud of the Bethune road, a rose in its rifle barrel and a cigarette behind its ear. So new was he to war that he still expected something fine and grand: heart-quickening music and flags flapping out in the breeze; for two days he had carefully buttoned up the skirts of his coat, out of the mud. He even believed that the rain would cease tomorrow. But tomorrow he too believed that all fighting troops had been thrust into purgatory for some unnamed sin, there to wait until some vague Being could decide what to do with them—to send them to hell or not.

A policeman passed, paused to stare at him, then moved on. And Jean-Baptiste shivered, clasping his jacket more closely about his throat. How many more policemen would see him, and move on? How many hours, minutes, seconds, before, at the flash of a shield or a heavy footfall, he must dart skulking into hiding? How much longer would he be free, to walk the earth and drink the sun— be uncaged? Perhaps tomorrow he would clasp steel bars like a caged ape, panting for freedom.

This is not fear, he cried to his soul. Had I known fear I would not have stolen fruit from the vicomte's garden, when I was young; I could not have done what I did at Souchez.

But what does this signify? Have not my wits extricated me before?

Yes, says caution. But who can break the chain of circumstance and forge a link so cunningly that none can tell? Who breaks laws and goes unscathed? Mine is mine, and thine is thine; and woe to him who would act otherwise. Think, too, of Pete; of this Tony the Wop: how long have you known them? Ten days. Can you say what a man whom you have known only ten days will do under a given circumstance? Can you say what you yourself will do under a given condition?

But what have I gained by being honest? Work, hard work, in a country foreign to my nature. America, the Golden Land, they tell us. And what have I got? Food and sleep.

What do you want?

I want to gain a part of that beauty which shall not pass from the earth, of companionship, of love, perhaps—who knows?

Aye, who knows? Who knows what he wants, even when he gains it? But do you expect to gain it by robbing banks?

Why not? Money is everything.

Certainly, money is everything. But only money you yourself have earned. Can you take money not yours and buy contentment with it? Can you gain strength and sustenance from the food eaten by someone else?

Ah, but money is different. The food has been eaten, but the money has not been spent.

Good! You have now reduced it to its personal equation. Could you eat all the food you could obtain at this moment?

No.

Have you ever been without food?

Yes, for four days.

But you ate again?

Obviously.

Then, do you not see that He who gave you food when it was necessary will also care for your other wants? Who are you, to assume charge of a vessel, the destiny of which you cannot know?

But this begs the question. Yours is a comfortable belief to die with, but I am not interested in death: it is
living I want; and life is more than food and sleep. So
this does not settle it.

There came footsteps sounding in the dark and empty
street, and Jean-Baptiste awoke from his problem. At last,
he thought, his problem would solve itself, once Pete and
the General came for him. But there was still time to
withdraw! No! he told himself; I have passed my word:
I will see it through. The danger was nothing, they had
told him. He spoke little English and he was known as
a quiet, law-abiding workman. But they could not understand that fear would not deter him, or that desire for
gain would [not] drive him into it. It was loneliness that
had done it: the quick despair of his hot Southern tem-
perament in an alien, heedless land.

But this was not Pete. A man passed carrying—of all
things—a saw. He stopped at the corner and Jean-Baptiste
cursed him: his mind was made up irrevocably. His five
years of labor among strange customs had netted him
nothing. Anything would be better than to continue in
the way he was living, anything! Let it be luxury or let
it be jail. He looked down the street again, waiting for
Pete and the General and Tony; his hands felt as cunning
and capable as separate organisms; the joy he had felt in
handling high explosive in a shell factory after he was
sorely wounded and incapacitated for action at the front,
returned seven fold. The old sinister joy of compounding
the volatile stuff, the benediction of a priest of the church
who had blessed an entire day's output—"Let these shells
scatter the enemies of France like chaff before the wind,
O Lord!"—recurred to him. To take destiny like a bit of

moist earth and mold a new man of it! Napoleon had done this—Napoleon, a round-headed, shrewd dreamer within whose veins ran the same fire, the same Southern sun, as in his.

Suddenly the empty street filled with sound, a resonant singing, half string and half pipe—a lilting provencal air somehow incongruously martial. Jean-Baptiste paused, stricken, and about him rose the land he called his; the wooded hills, and valleys, willow and tall chestnuts in the meadows where quiet cattle grazed or stood knee-deep in the water; of young love and nightingales among the chestnut trees after the sun had gone out of heaven and the intimate stars swam in a velvet sky. He saw the cottage where he was born, and ate and slept, sharp in the sun; he saw the wheeling candle light soft in a golden dusk beneath a single star like a yellow rose. He saw all this and knew that he had pursued a phantom into a far land; that destiny had taken him across seas so that he might see with a clear eye that thing which his heedless youth had obscured from him, which three years in the mud of Artois and Champagne could not make him see.

The strange yet familiar air rose and fell, and Jean-Baptiste lurched from his hiding place and went swiftly down the street. The musician sat on the curb, drawing his bow across his strange instrument; and so Jean-Baptiste passed swiftly on without disturbing him. At the end of the street the sky was rumorous with dawn, a new day.

Jealousy

———◆———

"**K**NITTING AGAIN, eh?"

His wife raised her smooth, oval face and her soft eyes for a moment met his, then dropped to her work again. "As you see, caro mio."

"Knitting! Always knitting! Is it that there is nothing to be done here that you must knit at all times?"

She sighed, but made no reply.

"Well?" he repeated, "cannot you speak? Have you lost your tongue?" he finished roughly.

"But it was you, 'Tono mio," she replied without raising her head, "who insist that I sit here instead of in my little red room, as I desired."

"Bah! Someone is needed here; would you have me pay wages to one that you might sit all day like a great lady, knitting with your gossips?"

A waiter, a tall young Roman god in a soiled apron, came between them and placed upon the desk a ticket and a bill. The woman made the change and gave the waiter a brief glance. He looked into her husband's face —a level stare in which his white satirical smile flashed, and withdrew. The other man's hand knotted into a fist upon the desk and he stared at his whitening knuckles as at something new and strange, cursing in a whisper. His wife raised her head and regarded him coldly.

"Don't be a fool, Antonio."

He controlled his voice by an effort. "How much longer will this continue?"

"Ah, that is what I would ask you: how much longer are you to vent your ill humor upon me?"

"You, with your demure face," he whispered fiercely, his hot little eyes blazing with bafflement and sudden rage.

She looked quickly about them. "Hush," she said, "people are looking. What do you want? Shall I withdraw to my room?"

His face was dreadful. "No," he shouted at last. He lowered his choking voice and continued: "I will not have it, do you hear?" He lowered his voice still more. "Listen. I will kill you, as I love God."

She picked up her knitting once more. "Don't be a fool," she repeated. "Return to your duties—see, patrons arrive. You are insane."

"Insane or not, do not drive me too far."

"You are insane: you talk, you scream, you curse— what?"

"You know well what."

"I? Have I ever given you cause or reason to go on so? Of what do you accuse me? Have I not been a good wife to you? Have I not at all times observed your wishes? You know well that I do not sit here night after night of my own wishes, of my own desires. This jealousy of yours is driving you mad."

"Bah! Be warned. That is all I say."

His gaze roamed from table to table as he sulked in his dirty apron, lurking among anaemic potted palms or serving his strange customers with servile insolence, and replying in snappish monosyllables to the greetings of old patrons. The tall, handsome waiter moved swiftly and deftly about, courteous and efficient. The husband compared the young man's supple grace with his own bulky figure and a fire gnawed in him. Once more the waiter approached the desk, his glance sweeping down the room rested briefly upon the husband's face, as he leaned intimately toward the wife.

The husband found himself walking in a red daze toward the two of them. He could not hear his own footfalls nor feel the floor beneath his feet. The waiter moved away as he approached, and his wife again sat bent above her knitting. Upon the desk was a china receptacle containing toothpicks; as he leaned upon the desk his fingers closed about the toothpick holder. The thing burst in his clenched hand amid a spurt of wooden splinters and a thin line of crimson was suddenly between his fingers and across the back of his hand.

"What did he say to you?" he asked; his voice to him seemed dry and light, like a broken egg shell.

The woman raised her head and her gaze met his full. Her eyes grew suddenly large, as though they would take up her whole face. "Listen," she said calmly, "you are insane. What would you have? Was it not you who put me here? I did not choose this." Her voice gathered warmth. "Am I to have no peace whatever? For six months now this has continued; day and night you have fretted and nagged at me; but now it must end. Either you come to your senses, or I leave you and return to my people. Take your choice: it is for you to make. But remember, this is the end. I have been a good wife to you, and I will still be if you but become again as you once were. But one more scene like this tonight, and I leave you."

He turned and walked away like a drunk man, or a somnambulist. He passed the waiter and the other's white, meaningless smile brought him to himself. He beckoned abruptly to the other and passed on through the kitchen and into a dark passage giving on an alley, where he waited, trembling. The waiter followed; in the constricted, shadowy place the other loomed above him, standing easily like a swordsman, looming above him though he was the bulkier man. Starlight was about them, and a faint wind stirred in the dingy alley.

"See," he said and his voice shook, "I know all; what is there between you?"

"Do you question me?" replied the other man.

"I will know: what is there between you?"

"There is nothing between us save the knowledge that you are crazy."

"Do not lie to me!"

" 'Lie?' This, to me? Do you give me the lie?" The younger man's body sprang like a poised sword, his fire seemed to make light the walls. The other quailed before him despite himself, cursing himself for his cowardice.

"But I must know! I will go mad!"

"You are already mad. Had you not been I should have killed you ere this. Listen, tub of entrails, there is nothing between us: for her sake whom you persecute, I swear it. I have said no word to her that you have not seen, nor she to me. If she be attracted to someone, it is not I. This I tell you because I am sorry for her, sorry for any woman who must be daily plagued by such as you."

"But what did you say to her but now, tonight?"

The young man slapped him, rocking his head upon his shoulders with two blows. The other staggered back. "I will kill you!" he screamed.

"You do not dare!" snapped the waiter, "you do not dare, save from behind. And what will the world say, if you do? Can you bear to have your wife call you coward? But I do not put this beyond you, hence I shall be on guard. And if you make the attempt, let it be successful, or God help you! Dog, and son of dogs!"

Alone again, the husband leaned against the cold alley wall panting, cursing in his rage and fear and hate. It was true: he did not dare. And he stared at the starred sky stretching like taut silk above the walled well of the alley, watching the same stars at which he had gazed in faraway Sicily, in his youth, when he had been a boy and life was clear and fine and simple; and that lads would stare wondering upon long after he and his dream and his problem were quiet underground.

He did not dare! The idea of assassination occurred to him, but he knew that he could not face himself afterward, his wife, that woman who had caused it all, whom he had taken but recently from her father's house and who was dearer to him than the world, than life itself, would never forgive him. He was almost middle-aged, and ugly and fat, while she, she was still young, and pretty. Was it any wonder that men were attracted to her as he had been? Was it any wonder that men should pause at her dusky oval face, her red mouth and raven hair, her black, black hair? And she—had she ever encouraged them? No! She had been a good wife to him, as she had said.

To go away, that was the answer—to take her to a new city; among new people they might yet live a second honeymoon. That was what he would do. He raised his face again to the heedless, flying stars among which his problem had got so interwoven and tangled; allowing the cool night air to play in his sweat-matted hair, and drew a long breath. That was the solution.

His wife agreed almost at once. They discussed the matter with her people and overcame their objections. She had informed her parents from time to time of his growing malady, so their decision did not surprise them. He was industrious and, until his present obsession took him, kind—a good husband in their eyes; too good to lose.

Once the decision made, he became his normal self again. In fact, things went so smoothly that he would have reconsidered, but his wife was firm. So a purchaser for the restaurant was found in the person of the tall young waiter. Relations between the two men were still strained and the older man avoided the other. Whenever they were forced to meet the younger acted as though nothing had happened. His white, sinister smile was the same as ever, yet the flash of his teeth in his dark face had somehow the power to enrage the other, stirring again in him old angers and fears he had thought asleep. But the waiter was more pleasant and courteous than ever; he insisted upon presenting the signora with a parting gift, with such a polite insistence that they could not refuse. And so at last, one day at noon, the two men set out to choose the gift.

A string of glass beads, or a medallion, the young man wanted. And they entered a curio shop where such things were sold—an orderless jumble of pictures, vases, bric-a-brac, jewelry, firearms and brass. While the waiter examined and haggled over his prospective purchase the older man stood idly near by. The purchaser stood near a window, a string of beads looping from his raised hand, oblivious and defenseless. And it occurred to the other that, for the first time the two of them had been together in the same room, his enemy was completely at his mercy. And while his hand groped behind him among a litter of ancient weapons his caution rebuked him for the thought. This had all been settled; he was going away tomorrow, perhaps never to see the man again. But it would be so easy! was the reply. Just to pretend that this old pistol fitting snugly in my palm were a modern, deadly machine—like this: and he slowly raised the rusted weapon while his thumb broke loose the hammer, and the spring which had slept for thirty years gathered itself. Like this! he whispered, aiming at the unconscious man he had once wanted to kill; and pulled the trigger.

The tiny room roared with sound and a lance of red flame leaped out like a sword. The young waiter crashed forward into a table of glassware, then to the floor; and the other man stood screaming with the burst pistol in his hand until a policeman plunged through the door.

Cheest

———◆———

C HEEST!

When he taken me out to look over them dogs he had
I says to him: "Say, whatcher doin'—startin' a glue factory?" I says. And he says, "Well, I dunno. I got a pay-
roll full of lads like you now, but all of you together
wouldn't make enough glue for one day's issue of thir-
teen-cent stamps. Bone fertilizer, mebbe, but not glue."

"Whatcher want," I comes back, "Jack Dempseys to
ride them dray horses?"

"Naw," he says, "what I want is a few riders without
no tongues. Then mebbe I can learn them something
about this business."

"Listen, fellow," I says, "they can't nobody tell me
nothing about the racing game."

"Nor about nothing else: I already seen that."

"Say," I says, looking him in the eye, "I'll quit you
cold, see?"

"That's fair enough; that's how I found you—cold and
broke, too."

"Say," I comes back, "you think you're smart, don't
you?"

"I got to be," he says, "or I'd been in the poorhouse ten years ago, with a stable full of beagles and clever children all eating their damn heads off."

Well, anyway we talked on back and forth, him not making nothing offa me—I been around, see? I have ridden the best in the land and I ain't had enough mud in my face to roon my complexion, neither. Ask anyone who's followed the game, suggest my name to them— Potter's the name, Jack Potter. Yeh.

Well, I thought I might's well stick with him, a while, anyway. So we worked out them dogs. Cheest, they was a terrible lot. They wasn't only one of them stood out at all, but them others was so orful that you could have tooken a horse out of a ice wagon and he would have showed class in that bunch. So I ast the boss to let me and a swipe see what we could do with him.

Well, he said all right, that even we couldn't make him no worse than he was, and something about a little child shall beat them to the wire or something—kind of kidding, see? He knowed I was a rider right away, only he wouldn't let on. That was his way, making out like I was like the rest of them alley rats or that his plugs would go to sleep at the post or get out in front and fall down. I seen through all his talk about us jocks, though between I and you they was a sorry bunch.

Well, to make a long story short, I meet this jane, see? I was to a movie one night by myself, and next to me was this kid and her friend, both skirts. Well, they was showing a racing fillum. Cheest, it was terrible. They was one horse looked like a winner, with a decent jock he could of walked away. But this bird riding him done everything he could, setting too far back and letting hisself be dragged along by the reins, letting another skate take the rail on him and break his stride.

"Cheest," I says kind of out loud, "if a jock of mine ever done that, I'd shoot him."

Well, these two kids setting next to me giggled, and I seen the blonde one looking me over. "Cheest," I says, "it gives me a pain to see a good horse butchered like that farmer done that one."

She kind of giggled again. Cheest, she was peachy looking, and when she ast me was I a racing man, why I kind of livened up, talking pretty wide, see? They expect it. Well, we was going pretty well, then she says: "Gee, listen at me talking to a stranger. Excuse me, mister." And she clams up. I introduced myself, saying I wasn't one of them birds goes around trying to make janes all the time, and so she thawed out and introduced her friend and her friend introduced her, and then everything was jake.

Well, anyway I bought them a soda after the show, and made a date with them for a couple nights later, me to bring a friend. And so I fixed it up with the least crummy of them rats I was with, and we met them like they said and taken them out. This was the night before the race we was cocked for, trying this here skate we had been working out. So we told them jellies we couldn't be out late account of something fixed at the track tomorrow, and they said that neither could they be out all night. They was nice girls, see, but good sports. Well, we was to a place dancing and joking and so forth, having a good time; and while my skirt wasn't looking, I taken one of her—you know—garters, see, kind of for luck or something.

Well, she kind of raised a howl about it, but I says: "Aw, come on, baby, soft pedal it. You wanna get us throwed out?"

"But how'm I gonna keep it up?" she wails.

"Roll it, kid, roll it," I says. "I ain't a smoking man or I'd do it for you."

"Like hell you would," she says, when this big bird comes over wanting to know what it's all about, saying they runs a decent place and won't have none of that stuff.

"Say," I says, "who you think you're talking to?"

"I ain't talking to nothing," he says. "I know your kind. And one more yap outa you, and the street for yours."

"You think you're smart, don't you?" I says, but he didn't have no comeback for that. So she goes to the ladies' dressing room and fixes herself, and we beat it. Believe me, I give that guy a look, too, but he wouldn't take it up.

Well, to make a long story short, when I dressed for the race the next day, I put this here garter on my arm, just for fun, see? Them skirts was coming out to see me ride. Well, the boss seen the garter on my arm and he says: "Whatcher got there, engagement ring?"

"Ah, go to hell," I says, and he seen I meant it and shut up.

They was a big crowd out that day, milling around and hollering their heads off for the favorite. Our horse was kind of nervous to begin with, and the bands and hollering never helped him none. He didn't look so bad, though, compared with them other platers. I got a good position, and everything looked pretty good.

We got away in fine shape, and that gang in the stands let out a howl, and that dog of mine busted out of the pack like he'd been doped. I held him in a little until the favorite—the best-looking one in the race—come up, then I stayed with him. I never worried at all about the others.

We was neck and neck at the half; at the three-quarters the other horse drawed ahead a little. The stands was whooping fit to kill, and the other jock went to the bat. Well, I let my baby out and we come down the stretch riding the best I knowed to get everything they was in him, and to make a long story short, I raised my whip and brang that dog in a half-length ahead.

The ones that had played us for a long shot was wild as Indians. Some of them busted out on the track and got drove back for their pains, but most of them run to collect while the ones that didn't have us watched them.

I weighed out, and there was the boss, with his hat cocked over one ear, feeling pretty good, I'll say.

"Well, I guess you're satisfied with my riding now," I says.

"Yes," he says, "you done your best, and still come in ahead, didn't you?"

Well, say! What do you know about that? And more'n that, he's had that damn garter sewed onto my shirt. And he ast me to find that jane so he could contract with her to furnish garters for all his riders.

Cheest!

Out of Nazareth

BENEATH the immaculate shapes of lamps we passed, between ancient softly greenish gates, and here was Jackson park. Sparrows were upon Andrew Jackson's head as, childishly conceived, he bestrode his curly horse in terrific arrested motion. Beneath his remote stare people gaped and a voice was saying: "Greatest piece of statuary in the world: made entirely of bronze, weighing two and a half tons, and balanced on its hind feet." And, thinking of how our great men have suffered at the hands of the municipal governments which they strove to make possible, pondering on how green the trees were, and the grass, and the narcissi and hyacinths like poised dancers; blessing that genius who conceived a park without any forbidden signs, where tramps could lie in the sun and children and dogs could pleasure themselves in the grass without reprimand; I remarked to Spratling how no one since Cezanne had really dipped his brush in light. Spratling, whose hand has been shaped to a brush as mine has (alas!) not, here became discursive on the subject of transferring light to canvas; but not listening to him I looked at the faces of old men sitting patiently on iron benches as we slowly paced—men who had learned that living is not only not passionate or joyous, but is not even especially sorrowful. One, in a worn frock coat and a new pair of tennis shoes, explained to me the virtue of tennis shoes and borrowed pipe tobacco from me. And then, beneath sparrows delirious in a mimosa, and a vague Diana in tortuous escape from marble draperies in the background, we saw him.

Hatless, his young face brooded upon the spire of the Cathedral, or perhaps it was something in the sky he was watching. Beside him was a small pack; leaning against his leg was a staff. Spratling saw him first. "My God," he said, clutching me, "look at that face."

And one could imagine young David looking like that. One could imagine Jonathan getting that look from David, and, serving that highest function of which sorry man is capable, being the two of them beautiful in similar peace and simplicity—beautiful as gods, as no woman can ever be. And to think of speaking to him, of entering that dream, was like a desecration.

His gray gaze returned to earth and he replied easily to our greeting. "Hello," he said. His voice, his speech was Middle Western; one thought of wheat slumbrous beneath a blue sky and a haze of dust, along the land; of long, peaceful lands where the compulsions of labor and food and sleep filled men's lives. But he could have come from anywhere, and he probably had. He was eternal, of the earth itself.

"Going far?" he asked him.

"I dunno: just looking around."

He was hungry, but there was nothing of the beggar in him. He reminded one of a pregnant woman in his calm belief that nature, the earth which had spawned him, would care for him, that he was serving his appointed ends, had served his appointed end and now need only wait. For what? He had probably never thought of it. As all the simple children of earth know, he knew that even poverty would take care of its own.

He had worked (always with his hands) and liked it— liked to feel a worn hoe or rake handle in his palm, or a pick handle. "It's like holding a new shoe in your hands," he explained to us, "and when you are tired and your arms kind of ache, but you have a few dollars in your pocket." He liked to sleep in hay better than in a bed, he told us; especially when the cattle stand there after dark, making "night sounds" and you can smell milk, sort of, and the ground, too.

This developed over lunch at Victor's. He ate frankly, like an animal and though he employed his cutlery as one should not, there was nothing offensive about it—it was exactly what he should have done.

No, he told Spratling, he hadn't seen many pictures. But some he liked, when there were people like you see every day in them, or trees. Especially trees. Trees were nicer than flowers, he thought.

"So you are a writer?" he asked me shyly. "Do you write like this book?" From his sorry jacket he drew a battered "Shropshire Lad" and as he handed it to me he quoted the one beginning, "Into my heart an air that kills—" telling us he kind of thought it was the best he had seen.

"Why don't you go home?" I asked him.

"I will, some day. But that ain't why I liked that one.

I like it because the man that wrote it felt that way, and didn't care who knew it."

"Is that so unusual?" I asked.

"Sir?"

"I mean, to feel something, and then write it exactly as you feel?"

Spratling here asked him if he had read Elizabeth Browning or Robert Frost. He had not—never heard of them. It seems that in Kentucky he had been given a meal in payment for which he had sawed wood; and, on leaving, a woman had asked him to throw away some old books and magazines. And among them he had found his "Shropshire Lad."

Again upon the street we had that feeling of imminence, of departure and a sundering of the cords of contact.

"But you will need money," I remarked.

Spratling interposed. "Come to me tomorrow at three. I can use you for a model."

"But I may not be here tomorrow," he objected.

"Then take some money," Spratling suggested.

"Thank you, sir," he replied. "I'll get along all right. Thank you both, mister, for the dinner."

"Don't be a fool," Spratling rejoined.

"No, sir, I'll be all right."

Mankind is never as complex as we would like to believe ourselves to be. And so I said: "We will give you a dollar, and tomorrow you come to this address."

"But, mister, I am not begging: I don't need your money. I will have a job by night."

"No, no; take the money, and call on us tomorrow."

"Why, I can get a job any time."

"Surely," Spratling replied, "but I want you to come to me tomorrow afternoon."

"But, mister, I may not be here."

"But won't you come, as a favor?"

His gaze brooded down Chartres street. "I guess I can. But I had rather give you something for the money." He turned to me. "Here, you are a writing man. I will give you this, and if I ain't there, you can have this for the dollar."

And this is what he gave me. There is bad punctuation here, and misspelling: there is one word I have never deciphered. But to correct it would ruin it.

AN OPEN ROAD stretching into the distance. Long lines of fences heming it in. Back of the fields, low hills in the distance. Not big hills but rolling formations overhung by a blue haze.

Cars whizz by. Cars filled with touring families. Cars with a single occupant. Delapidated Fords in which farmers drive to town. Cars filled with family parties bound to visit relatives in some nearby town.

With a pack on my back (consisting of necessary articles rolled in two blankets) I trudge along. The smell of farm house fires drifts down the wind to me. Pure air fills my lungs and gives an exhileration unlike any other that I know. The morning sun casts long shadows accross the fields. The dew of early morning glitters and the tall grass overhanging the side of the road is heavy with it. I am at peace with the world. Nothing matters.

I have eaten at a little restaurant. I have slept well on dried corn stalks between long rows of corn. I need not travel. I have no destination. I am at peace with the world.

I have my thoughts as a companion. Days spent alone have given me the habit of talking aloud to myself. Roosters crow, birds sing, a crow slowly wings his way from one distant wood clump to another. I seem to be in true communion with nature.

As the sun creeps higher the glare of summer is reflected from long rows of yellow corn. The road glistens and is a white streak which has no definite end at the horrizon. I sweat. Great drops roll down my face and settle in my open collar. The heat is good. It loosens the legs and warms the ground for the night's sleep.

Miles slide behind me. Now and again a car stops and I am given a ride. I do not ask for it. Why should I ask for rides when all around me is content? Those who wish to help me may do so, others may go on their way. I have no destination. Why should I hurry?

Noon comes and I lunch frugally on soup and milk. The hills that were before me this morning now surround me. The road no longer runs straight, but winds and dips among them. Trees overhang it and give a welcome shade from the noonday sun. Nature seems to plan my protection.

All afternoon I loll on the back seat of a speeding car (who's owner had invited me to ride). There is a dog in the back seat with me and we converse together as best we may. I scratch his ears and he cocks his head to one side and wags his tail. I stop for a minute to watch the changing form of some hill and he gently nudges me with his nose. My hand returns to his head and we resume our camradie.

The sun sinks lower and is hidden beyond the hill. There is still plenty of time to find a camp. We come to a busy hill town and my heaviest meal is eaten. The food tastes as only food can taste to an appetite sharpened by a day spent in constant motion in the open air.

A slow tramp through the main street of the town and through the residential district brings me to the city camp. As I walk I look at the people restting on the porches, reading, talking and basking in the pleasant thought of a full day gone. Farther out I come to a region of stoops. Here shoeless laborers sit against buildings, one foot propped on a knee, smoking and talking shop, sports and politics. I catch words, sentences, fragments as I swing along.

Now and again a party sitting on a stoop stops its conversation to look at me. Perhaps a voice calls, "Where you from, kid?" and another, "Where you going?"

At the camp I find a place as far as possible from the rows of tents and spread my blankets. I wash my socks, which have become caked with sweat and the dust from the road. I brush my teeth and bathe as best I can.

I would ordinarily prefer to sleep in an open field or in a sheltering wood away from people. But tonight I desire the society of my own kind, so I stroll through the camp exchanging road gossip, stories, experiences, with motherly fat women washing dishes, wandering workers, business men out for a change, or a group of young men off for somewhere. Perhaps I help one of the women with her dishes and am rewarded with breakfast the next morning.

As it grows dark the fires stand out. The white walls of the tents reflect the light through, some music starts up and a party of young people start a dance on the porch of the small general store which serves the wants of the campers.

At the dance no introductions are necessary. We are all brothers and sisters. We are members of the fraternity of the open road, some for a short time, others forever.

Friendships develop quickly. Here is a German doctor [*sic*], a curious twisted little person with his hat on one side, playing some card game with a young Swede from the Dakotas who, it is evident, has lived in this country but a short time. The actor is going to the West to try the movies, the Swede is out to see the country. When he uses up his money he will sell his car and go to work.

A thin-faced, gangling Arkansan is discurrsing to several silent Westerners his difficulties in the Northwest. His youngest son, a boy of nine years, says to a playmate, "We pritt' nigh been all ova the country. We was in Vancouvar through California. We air headin' for the East now, and we'll get there prit' soon if Pop don't haf' to stop and get a job carpentering to buy us gas and food."

I HAVE given his story word for word, as he wrote it. The spelling I have not changed, nor the punctuation. Some of the words mean nothing, as far as I know (and words are my meat and bread and drink), but to change them would be to destroy David himself. And so I have given it as it was given to me: blundering and childish and "arty," and yet with something back of it, some impulse which caused him to want to write it out on paper. And who knows? Give him time. He confided to Spratling and me, blushing, that he is seventeen.

But seeing him in his sorry clothes, with his clean young face and his beautiful faith that life, the world, the race, is somewhere good and sound and beautiful, is good to see.

He would not promise to call upon us. "You see, I wrote this, and I liked it. Of course it ain't as good as I wisht it was. But you are welcome to it." His young face stared into an ineffable sky, and the sun was like a benediction upon him.

"You see," he told us, "I can always write another one."

The Kingdom of God

———◆———

THE CAR came swiftly down Decatur street and turning into the alleyway, stopped. Two men alighted, but the other remained in his seat. The face of the sitting man was vague and dull and loose-lipped, and his eyes were clear and blue as cornflowers, and utterly vacant of thought; he sat a shapeless, dirty lump, life without mind, an organism without intellect. Yet always in his slobbering, vacuous face were his two eyes of a heart-shaking blue, and gripped tightly in one fist was a narcissus.

The two who had got out of the car leaned within it and went swiftly to work. Soon they straightened up, and a burlap bundle rested on the door of the car. A door in the wall near at hand opened, a face appeared briefly and withdrew.

"Come on, let's get this stuff out of here," said one of the men. "I ain't scared, but there ain't no luck in making a delivery with a loony along."

"Right you are," replied the other. "Let's get done here: we got two more trips to make."

"You ain't going to take him along, are you?" asked

the first speaker, motioning with his head toward the one lumped oblivious in the car.

"Sure. He won't hurt nothing. He's a kind of luck piece, anyway."

"Not for me he ain't. I been in this business a long time and I ain't been caught yet, but it ain't because I been taking no squirrel chasers for luck pieces."

"I know how you feel about him—you said so often enough. But like it was, what could I do? He never had no flower, he lost it somewheres last night, so I couldn't leave him to Jake's, going on like he was for another one; and after I got him one today I couldn't of put him out nowheres. He'd of stayed all right, till I come for him, but some bull might of got him."

"And a —— good thing," swore the other. "Dam'f I see why you lug him around when they's good homes for his kind everywheres."

"Listen. He's my brother, see? And it's my business what I do with him. And I don't need no —— that wears hair to tell me, neither."

"Ah, come on, come on. I wasn't trying to take him away from you. I'm just superstitious about fooling with 'em, that's all."

"Well, don't say nothing about it, then. If you don't wanta work with me, say so."

"All right, all right, keep your shirt on." He looked at the blind doorway. "Cheest, what's the matter with them birds today? Hell, we can't wait here like this: be better to drive on. Whatcher say?" As he spoke the door opened again and a voice said: "All right, boys."

The other gripped his arm, cursing. At the corner two blocks away a policeman appeared, stood a moment, then sauntered down the street toward them. "—— here comes a bull. Make it snappy now; get one of them fellows inside to help you and I'll head him off and keep him till you get unloaded." The speaker hurried off and the other, glancing hurriedly about, grasped the sack resting upon the door of the car and carried it swiftly through the doorway. He returned and leaned over the side of the car, trying to lift up the other sack onto the door. The policeman and his companion had met and were talking.

Sweat broke out on his face as he struggled with the awkward bundle, trying to disengage it from the floor of the car. It moved, but hung again despite his utmost efforts, while the body of the car thrust against his lower chest, threatened to stop his breathing. He cast another glance toward the officer. "What luck, what rotten luck!" he panted, grasping the sack again. He released one hand and grasped the idiot's shoulder. "Here, bub," he whispered, "turn around here and lend a hand, quick!" The other whimpered at his touch, and the man hauled him half about so that his vacant, pendulous face hung over the back seat. "Come on, come on, for God's sake," he repeated in a frenzy, "catch hold here and lift up, see?"

The heavenly blue eyes gazed at him without intent, drops of moisture from the drooling mouth fell upon the back of his hand. The idiot only raised his narcissus closer to his face. "Listen!" the man was near screaming, "do you wanta go to jail? Catch hold here, for God's sake!" But the idiot only stared at him in solemn detachment, and the man raised up and struck him terribly in the face. The narcissus, caught between fist and cheek, broke and hung limply over the creature's fist. He screamed, a hoarse, inarticulate bellow which his brother, standing beside the officer, heard and came leaping toward him.

The other man's rage left him and he stood in vacant and frozen despair, when vengeance struck him. The brother leaped, shrieking and cursing, upon him and they both went to the pavement. The idiot howled unceasingly, filling the street with dreadful sound.

"Hit my brother, would you, you ——," panted the man. The other, after the surprise of the assault, fought back until the policeman leaped upon them, clubbing and cursing impartially. "What in hell is this?" he demanded when they were erect and dishevelled, glaring and breathless.

"He hit my brother, the ——."

"Somebody certainly done something to him," snapped the officer. "For Pete's sake, make him stop that racket," he roared above the deafening sound. Another policeman thrust through the gathering crowd. "What you got here? Mad cow?" The idiot's voice rose and fell on waves of unbelievable sound and the second policeman, stepping to the car, shook him.

"Here, here," he began, when the brother, breaking from the grasp of his captor, leaped upon his back. They crashed against the car, and the first officer, releasing the other captive, sprang to his aid. The other man stood in amazement, bereft of power to flee, while the two officers swayed and wrestled with the brother, stretching the man, screaming and kicking, between them until he wore himself out. The second policeman had two long scratches on his cheek. "Phew!" he puffed, mopping his jaw with his handkerchief, "what a wildcat! Has the whole zoo broke out today? What's the trouble?" he roared above the magnificent sorrow of the idiot.

"I dunno exactly," his partner shouted back. "I hear that one in the car bellow out, and look around and here's these two clawing in the gutter. This one says the other one hit his brother. How about it?" he ended, shaking his captive.

The man raised his head. "Hit my brother, he did. I'll kill him for this!" he shouted in a recurrence of rage, trying to cast himself on the other prisoner, who crouched behind the other policeman. The officer struggled with him. "Come on, come on; want me to beat some sense into you? Come on, make that fellow in the car stop the howling."

The man looked at his brother for the first time. "His flower is broken, see?" he explained, "that's what he's crying about."

" 'Flower?' " repeated the law. "Say, what is this, anyway? Is your brother sick, or dead, that he's got to have a flower?"

"He ain't dead," interjected the other policeman, "and he don't sound sick to me. What is this, a show? What's going on here?" He peered into the car again and found the burlap sack. "Aha," he said. He turned swiftly. "Where's the other one? Get him quick! They've got liquor in here." He sprang toward the second man, who had not moved. "Station house for yours, boys." His companion was again struggling with the brother, and he quickly handcuffed his captive to the car, and sprang to the other's aid.

"I ain't trying to get away," the brother was shrieking.

"I just want to fix his flower for him. Lemmego, I tell you!"

"Will he quit that bellowing if you fix his flower?"

"Yeh, sure; that's what he's crying for."

"Then for God's sake fix it for him."

The idiot still clutched his broken narcissus, weeping bitterly; and while the officer held his wrist the brother hunted about and found a small sliver of wood. String was volunteered by a spectator, who fetched it from a nearby shop; and under the interested eyes of the two policemen and the gathering crowd, the flower stalk was splinted. Again the poor damaged thing held its head erect, and the loud sorrow went at once from the idiot's soul. His eyes were like two scraps of April sky after a rain, and his drooling face was moonlike in ecstasy.

"Beat it, now," and the officers broke up the crowd of bystanders. "Show's all over for the day. Move on, now."

By ones and twos the crowd drifted away. And with an officer on each fender the car drew away from the curb and on down the street, and so from sight, the ineffable blue eyes of the idiot dreaming above his narcissus clenched tightly in his dirty hand.

The Rosary

———————◆———————

M̲R. HARRIS hated two things: his neighbor, Juan Venturia, and a song called "The Rosary." He took a fierce delight in never having been able to decide which he hated most. On those days when Venturia, cleaning his premises, dumped trash and tin cans—and once a dead cat—into Mr. Harris' areaway; or when one of Mr. Harris' prized chickens got onto Venturia's premises and suffered abrupt and complete extinction in consequence, he knew that he hated Venturia with a passion unknown to this world. But, when forced by his wife or daughters to attend one of those musical functions where foreigners with uncurried manes who could neither speak nor play in English, scraped dolefully away at fiddles, he knew that nothing anywhere could be worse than "The Rosary"—or any other tune, as far as he was concerned.

Juan Venturia, on his part, neither knew nor cared a whoop in hades about "The Rosary." He was unmarried, hence he didn't have to attend concerts, which served to make Mr. Harris more furious than ever. He thought the police should do something about it. Venturia found life good: there was money to be made, he met his friends nightly at a certain restaurant, he went and came as he liked. So he could save all his hatred for Mr. Harris and Mr. Harris' chickens, and his cat and his house, and everything that Mr. Harris owned or liked.

Life was indeed good. He could watch for Mr. Harris and whistle "The Rosary" while the other passed, he answered advertisements in magazines, having samples of mange and tobacco cures, toilet articles, cooking utensils, etc., sent to Mr. Harris C.O.D., and then sat in his chair and heard Mr. Harris rave terribly and in vain.

One day Mr. Harris did not appear at his usual hour; and Venturia, being unable to whistle "The Rosary" as he passed, felt that his enemy had deliberately injured him. But when he heard later that Mr. Harris was ill, he was suffused with glee. For a whole day he sat chuckling in his shop, breaking occasionally into shouts of laughter, to the consternation of his patrons. At the cafe that evening he was gay and merry, keeping his companions in roars of laughter.

Later, as he lay in bed, heaving and chuckling, a terrible thought struck him. Suppose his enemy were to die! Be beyond the reach of his hatred! He thought of all the chances of really doing something mean to Mr. Harris, and his joy left him. Just killing a few dirty yellow chickens and throwing a little garbage into his areaway—what were these, compared to what he might have done? Nothing, and less than nothing. These tricks were childish, a ten-year-old boy could have thought of these. But he, Venturia, was a man: he should have thought of something to have driven his foe to bed and made him long to die. And now, it was too late. His enemy was beyond his reach, there was nothing he could do to injure him. He cursed himself, racking his brains.

To let his enemy escape like this! If Mr. Harris died he, Venturia, would be miserable: he would be forced to die also and follow the other to purgatory and so finish the business which he had criminally neglected in life. If there were but something, anything, he could do before his foe foiled him forever by dying! He tossed and turned, sleeping fitfully and waking again to groan and mourn his lost opportunities. How many things he could think of now, when it was too late! He could still set fire to Mr. Harris' house, but this meant the risk of imprisonment. Hence part of his despairing rage was transferred to the police. Chance, government, everything was against him. . . .

He waked suddenly from a fragmentary dream. Dawn was grayly at the window. A wagon rattled past and a ship bellowed hoarsely from the river. Venturia sprang from his bed, stifling a cry of victory. He had it at last: he had dreamed it. So simple it was, and so grand! It would make his enemy pant for death; it was colossal. There was only one flaw in it. "Why, oh why, did I not think of this before?" he moaned. "I could have driven him crazy, I could have made him as an idiot, mewling and weeping, beating his head upon the floor!"

He would have run from his house to accomplish it immediately, then his calm sense returned. So he crawled back in his bed and lay nursing his scheme in fiendish, impatient glee, until morning came. He made a hurried breakfast, locked his shop, and hastened up Royal street, like one possessed. Before a pawnshop he paused, then disappeared within it. A few minutes later he reappeared carrying a longish, bulky object wrapped in newspaper under his arm. He turned off Royal street in the opposite direction from his shop, and all that day his shop remained locked and closed, and for a week his old haunts knew him not.

Mr. Harris lay at home in the throes of pneumonia. In the intervals of consciousness he found time to wonder what Venturia was doing, what he was up to. He knew the other would not let him alone to die in peace. He expected anything, something violent in the way of noise, whatever his enemy's childlike mind could conceive. But day after day passed, and nothing happened, and Mr. Harris became a trifle fretful over it. It was like waiting for an explosion which for some reason is delayed, expecting it each moment and flinching, until even the explosion becomes preferable.

"Wish he'd get it over with," thought the sick man fretfully. "But it won't be long," he reassured himself. "I'm about gone, and the beast can't get at me much longer, thank heaven. And thank heaven, I won't have to attend any more concerts. Death ain't so bad, after all," mused Mr. Harris, like many a man before him.

And what of Venturia? Those companions whom he was wont to meet and who saw him no longer, asked this question among themselves. But no one had seen him. His shop saw but little of him, and when he was in he sat staring raptly at the wall, his hands held stiffly before him one above the other at the height of his belt, while his dirty fingers waggled stiffly as though in some clumsy, yet intricate sign language. And passersby stared in amazement and the little blackguard boys with pleasure, at his intent, corrugated face and the rigid genuflections of his hands. At twilight he closed his shop, and carrying his lumpy bundle, he left, returning about midnight to sleep and chuckle and dream of his revenge.

At last came the day. Now that the hour was come all Venturia's excitement was gone. He was calm, awaiting his destiny. He rose, breakfasted leisurely, shaved and donned his Sunday suit and a white shirt. He shined his shoes and plastered his hair to his head with scented oil. Then picking up his bundle he repaired to his areaway directly beneath the window where he knew the sick man lay.

He raised his eyes and gloated upon the dumb wall of his enemy's house. It seemed to him that his gaze could pierce the walls, that he was in the very room where the other lay. Then, slowly, he unwrapped the soiled and tattered newspaper from his engine of vengeance.

Mr. Harris, though, was no longer in that room. His wife was there, and his daughters were there, beside the bed where Mr. Harris had lain and waited for whatever Venturia might decide to perpetrate next; but Mr. Harris himself had gone where the Venturias of the world could not bother him more, where slain chickens and even dead cats in his areaway were of no importance.

From beneath the window there rose suddenly the excruciating, succulent bray of a saxophone blown by a rank amateur. The tune seemed to be nothing, the tune seemed to be two tunes played at the same time: it blatted and mewed and wept, filling the morning and spilling the dusty sparrows tumultuously from the eaves.

Only Venturia and Mr. Harris could have known that it was "The Rosary."

The Cobbler

You wan' getta thees shoe today? Si, si. Yes, I coma from—tella in my tongue? Buono signor.

Yes, I come from Tuscany, from the mountains, where the plain is gold and brown in the barren sun, and the ancient hills brood bluely above the green and dreaming valleys. How long? Ah, who knows? I am very old: I have forgotten much.

When I was young I lived much in the sun, tending goats. The people of my village labored among the vineyards sprawled upon the slopes drinking up the sun; as I followed my flocks I could see them, the bright colors, and hear the faint, sweet singing like the broken flight of golden birds. I munched my bread and cheese at noon, and drowsed among the sun-swelled rocks until the air and heat and silence sent me to swim in warm slumber. And always at sunset an ancient father of goats roused me with his cold nose.

And she was young also. Almost daily we met among the hills, I with my goats and she having slipped away from her set tasks, to idle in the sweet sun. How like a little goat she was, leaping chasms at which I paused, taking what pleasure the day offered, knowing that punishment awaited her for slipping away, knowing that she could slip away again on the morrow. And so it was.

And ah, how she bloomed; how, when we both became older, how the eyes of the young men did follow her. But I had not been idle: I had labored, I had goats of my own; and so we were promised: it was all arranged. She no longer climbed the morning hill with me now. She must remain at home, baking and making cheeses of goats' milk, treading out the grapes in the autumn, staining her sweet white feet with the sunned purple juice, as though the dear Christ Himself had bathed her feet in His own dear blood, as I would gladly have done.

And on the feast days, in her scarlet kerchief, how she shone among the others! Her tossing hair in the dance, her sweet wild breasts arbored amid her hair! It is no wonder, signor, that the young men panted and wept for her, for where in our valley, in all the world, was her equal? But we were promised: it was all arranged.

After the fiddles were silent and the sun had dropped beyond the dreaming purple hills and the bells chimed across the dusk like the last golden ray of the sun broken and fallen echoed among the rocks, we often walked. The belled flocks were stilled and candles guttered gold about the supper tables, and we walked hand in hand while the stars came out so big, so near—it is not like that in your America, signor.

She often chided me on my backwardness in the dance or with the girls—how I labored and saved, and at the dancing looked but diffidently on while others danced and wooed her in their colored shirts and copper flashing rings. And she often teased me, saying that one of her beauty deserved better than I. With which I agreed, for where in our valley was her equal? But we were promised.

Am I married? No, signor. The saints had willed otherwise. She? . . . . (I am old: I forget easily.) Ah. There was one came to our village: a grand signor in velvet and with rings of pure gold—like a lord he was, with his dark, proud look, like a thin sword in a velvet sheath. He, too, saw her upon the green, saw her like a sweet music one has forgot, and he, too, became as the other young men. And she, when she saw that grand one with eyes for none save her, she danced as none of that village had ever danced. They who watched were hushed as though they had looked briefly into heaven, for she was like the music of a hundred fiddles become one white and scarlet flame, she was like to make the sleeping saints in heaven wake sad, and know not why. But what would you? He wore velvet, and his rings were of pure gold. But then, we were promised.

That night, amid the hills where I walked, the great stars were loud as bells in the black sky, loud as great golden-belled sheep cropping the hill of heaven, like the great old ones among goats who had seen much sorrow, and still browsed on. But soon the night was gone away, and the stars were gone, and the hills were azure and gold in the morning. And there, in the dust beneath her window, where I was wont to pause briefly of a morning, was this yellow rose. It was not then as it is now: now it is old and black and twisted, as I am; but then it was green and fresh and young. Yes, I have kept it. When she returns she will doubtless desire me to have kept it;

had I not kept it, she will be sad. And it has well repaid me: yearly it renews itself—like this. The saints are very good.

What? Was I sad? I do not know. I have known joy and sorrow, but now I do not remember. I am very old: I have forgotten much.

You getta thees shoe today. Si, si.

Chance

————◆————

HIS ROUND, fatuous face was smug with self-esteem. He had completely forgotten that he had not wherewith to buy his next meal: why should he? The Lord will provide. And now with his cuffs turned and his collar on wrong side out, his shabby suit shaken into something resembling its former shape, why should he? He looked as good as any of them.

"Mebbe they'll think I'm a racing man, with a roll on my hip would choke a ox," he said to himself, sneaking looks at his passing image in the shop windows. Nowhere on Royal street could he see another flat that looked as good as he did. He took another long look at himself in a window, and collided with another body.

"Listen, brother," this one began, "I ain't ate since three days ago. Can't you gimme the price of a cup of coffee? Listen, I been drunk: I admit it; but now I'm trying to sober up, see? How about a cup of beefstew to sober up on? God will see it from heaven, and He'll reward you, guy."

"Hell," he replied, "you can't buy a drink here for two bits, can you?"

His new friend became expansive. "Why, sure, if you've got the price. Listen, I can take you to a nice quiet family place, where I'm well known, see? Anybody I bring there is all right. Of course you've got to have the price."

He took the other's arm; and the beggar drooped upon him affectionately. "Let's go," he said.

They had a drink.

There were two other guests present, a truck driver and a very ex something that smacked vaguely of the sea, who joined him. "Let her ride," he said, with that grandeur only to be achieved by one with brass and no money.

They had another—three of them did. The beggar was ignored this time, and he immediately became vocal.

"Come on, men," he said, "lemme in on this. I'll buy a round—see if I don't."

"We can't wait that long," murmured the truck driver, and the beggar became insistent.

"Listen," he said, grasping his patron's arm, "listen. Who brought you here? Who showed you the most convenient place in New Orleans? I did. And yet you let your rich friends treat me like I was a dog or something. Listen, I'm a self-respecting seaman waiting for a berth. Sure, I ain't got any money, but I wouldn't treat a dog like you're treating me. Jest one drink, men, before I go down to the shipping office." He pawed his benefactor with passion.

"Get to hell away from me," said that hero, flinging him off violently. The beggar fell, and got slowly to his feet; and as the other turned again to the bar, leaped upon his back. They went down together; he rose and tried sincerely to kick the beggar's head off, but the two of them were grasped and ejected bodily into the street. They sat up, under the disgusted stare of a policeman.

He stated his case to a bored desk sergeant; the beggar stated his case, aloud and still louder.

"My God," broke in the sergeant, "get 'em out of here. I can't stand this any longer."

"Where to, sergeant?" asked the patrolman. His sister had not got married the night before.

"Anywhere!" roared the official, "just so they can't talk to me any longer."

So once more he found himself in the gutter. He sat for a while stupidly staring at the blank door of the station. His hand rested on something round and hard: he closed his fingers on it and raised it from the mud. In his hand was a penny—a copper cent.

A copper cent. What in the world could you buy with a copper cent? Why, chewing gum, provided he could find one of those gum vending machines; or he could get weighed for a cent; or he could buy a box of matches for it. So he picked himself up, wiping the mud from his clothes. Alas! he no longer looked as if he might have a roll on him.

As he approached Canal street, looking for a gum vending machine, a running man plunged by him, followed by an excited chase crying "Stop thief!"

He joined the pursuit, and the fleeing man sped past a corner. A cop stepped out; they collided and the quarry went down. The policeman grasped his collar before he could rise. The pursuit panted up.

"What's going on here?" asked the law.

A breathless pursuer explained.

"This feller stole a five-dollar goldpiece from a news-paper seller. He took a paper, put down a nickel, and picked up a penny and a five-dollar goldpiece the boy had on his shelf."

The policeman shook his captive. "How about it, huh?"

"Honest, officer," the man pleaded, "I never meant to take his money. I picked it up by mistake, and just as I was about to tell him about it, he falls backward into the gutter and starts hollering 'Stop thief!' And I ran before I thought."

"Have you still got it?"

"Sure: here it is. I was going to give it back to him. Honest, I ain't no thief: I got a job here in town—lived here all my life."

The officer looked at the gathering crowd. "Where's the newsboy?" he asked, and his eye fell on our hero. "You, there, with the mud on you: is this your gold-piece?"

He felt himself thrust forward, and the original informant averred: "Sure, officer, this is the one."

The policeman examined our hero narrowly. "I'm a good mind to take you both up, but this bird"—shaking his captive—"says it was a mistake. Whatcher wanna do? Have him arrested, or take your money back and let him go?"

"I'll take the five," he replied, and the crowd murmured approbation.

The culprit passed over the goldpiece.

"Here, here," the policeman interjected, "you owe him a penny yet."

From his muddied clothes he took the penny he had

found and gave it to the other. The crowd melted away, as such crowds do, and he was left staring at the five-dollar goldpiece in his hand.

Five dollars. What to do with five dollars? He thought immediately of five dollars' worth of food. But it would be foolish to spend gold money for food when there were so many other ways of getting food. This seemed to be his lucky day, anyhow. His lucky day . . . . his lucky day. . . .

When your luck is good, why, force it. Any fool knows that. And there, on a billboard on Canal street, was a list of today's entries. And in the third race was a horse named Penny Wise. It was a portent: an indication from the very gods that run the world. So he put his five on Penny Wise at forty to one. And Penny Wise broke out of the whole field like a scared rabbit.

Two thousand dollars. What couldn't you buy with two thousand dollars? He sat in a park, trying to recall all the things he had once wanted. Funny how when you're broke you can think of any number of things you'd like to buy, but as soon as you have the price you can't recall to save your life what it was. "So I guess I'll buy a car," he said. "Mebbe that's what I want."

"Listen," a friend said to him, "lemme take that money for you. You'll run through it in a month, and then you'll be on the street again. Lemme take care of it for you."

"Sure," he said; and had his clothes cleaned and pressed for eighty-five cents; and he bought a lemon-colored sports car for one thousand nine hundred and eighty-nine dollars. A kind salesman undertook to teach him to drive it. He caught on quite fast—so fast that he drove out Jackson avenue and off the Jackson avenue dock into the river at about forty miles an hour. The salesman leaped to safety; he followed suit and so suffered only a skinned knee. But he was close enough to see the grand and mournful splash his car made in the muddy water.

The shore-coming crew of a tramp steamer cursed him; and as he stood watching the spreading ripples a hand fell on his shoulder. He had been arrested for speeding.

After paying street car fare for himself and the optimistic salesman he had ten dollars and one cent. His fine for speeding was ten dollars.

He stood for a moment stupidly staring at [the] blank door of the station. In his hand was something round and hard; he closed his fingers on it and raised it from his pocket. In his hand was a penny—a copper cent.

He threw it into the mud of the gutter and walked on up the street, his round, fatuous face smug with self-esteem. Perhaps people would think he was a racing man, with a roll on his hip would choke an ox.

Sunset

———◆———

Black Desperado Slain

The negro who has terrorized this locality
for two days, killing three men, two whites
and a negro, was killed last night with
machine gun fire by a detachment of
the –th Regiment, State National Guard.
The troopers set up their gun before the
copse in which the black was hiding and
when there was no reply to their fire,
Captain Wallace entered the place and
found the negro dead. No reason has been
ascertained for the black's running amuck,
though it is believed he was insane. He
has not been identified.
—The Clarion-Eagle.

————————

H E CAME part of the way on or in or beneath
freight cars, but mostly he walked. It took him two days
to come from Carrollton avenue to Canal street, because
he was afraid of the traffic; and on Canal street at last,
carrying his shotgun and his bundle, he stood frightened
and dazed. Pushed and shoved, ridiculed by his own
race and cursed by policemen, he did not know what to
do save that he must cross the street.

So at last, taking his courage in both hands and shutting his eyes, he dashed blindly across in the middle of the block. Cars were about him, a taxi driver screamed horrid imprecations at him, but, clutching his gun and bundle, he made it. And then a kind white man directed him to the river which he sought.

And here was a boat, all tied up to the bank, waiting for him. In climbing down a pile and leaping six feet of water to get on it, he nearly lost his gun; and then another white man, cursing, drove him from the boat.

"But, cap'n," he protested, "I jest wants to go to Af'ica. I kin pay my way."

"Africa, hell," said the white man. "Get to hell off this boat. If you ever try to get on here again that way I'll shoot you. Get on up yonder and get a ticket, if you want to ride."

"Yes, suh. 'Scuse me, cap'n."

"What?" repeated the ticket seller, in amazement.

"Lemme have a ticket to Af'ica, please um."

"Do you mean Algiers?"

"No'm; Af'ica."

"Do you want a ferry ticket?"

"Yassum, I expec' so: so I kin ride dat boat waitin' yonder."

"Come on, come on, up there," said a voice from the waiting queue behind him, so he took his ticket and was hustled through the gate and was once more on board the ferry.

To his surprise the boat, instead of going down the river, in which direction he vaguely supposed Africa to be, held straight across the stream, and he was herded ashore like a sheep. Clinging to his gun he stared about

him helplessly. At last he diffidently approached a policeman.

"Cap'n, suh, is dis Af'ica?"

"Huh?" said the startled officer.

"Ah'm tryin' to get to Af'ica, please suh. Is dis de right
way?"

"Africa, hell," said this white man, just as the steamboat
man had done. "Look here, what are you up to?"

"Ah wants to go back home, whar de preacher say us
come fum."

"Where do you live, nigger?"

"Back up yonder ways, in de country."

"What town?"

"Ain't no town, suh, 'ceptin' Mist' Bob and de fambly
and his niggers."

"Mississippi or Louisiana?"

"Yessuh, I 'speck so."

"Well, lemme tell you something. You go back there
on the first train you can catch. This ain't no place for
you."

"But, cap'n, I wants to go to Af'ica."

"You forget about Africa, and go buy yourself the
longest railroad ticket you can, do you hear?"

"But, cap'n—"

"Beat it, now. Do you want me to take you up?"

At the foot of Canal street again, he looked about him
in perplexity. How did one get to Africa? He was hustled and shoved this way and that, and he allowed destiny
to carry him along the river front. Here was another
boat tied up to the wharf, with niggers carrying things
up a plank and dumping them down upon the floor. A
coatless white man was evident, loudly.

Niggers pushing trucks rattled and banged, singing, about him. He was still thrust around, leaping from the path of one truck only to find another bearing down upon him. "Look out, black man!"

Suddenly the boss whirled upon him.

"What in hell are you doing? Grab aholt of something there, or get off this job. I don't have no spectators on this job at all. You hear me."

"Yas suh, cap'n," he returned equably; and soon he was throwing sacks onto a truck. His blood warmed with activity, he began to sweat and to sing. This was where he was at home—for the first time in how long? He had forgotten. "Af'ica, where is you?" he said.

Quitting time: the sun hung redly in the west and the long shadows were still and flat, waiting for dark. The spinning golden motes spun slower in the last sunlight; and the other hands gathered up coats and lunch pails and moved away toward the flashing street lights, and supper. He picked up his gun and bundle and went aboard the boat.

Among soft, bulky sacks he lay down to munch the loaf of bread he had bought. Darkness came down completely, the lapping of water against the hull and the pungently sweet smell of the sacked grain soon put him to sleep.

Motion waked him, a smooth lift and fall and a steady drumming of engines. Light was about him and he lay in a dullness of comfort, not even thinking. Then he found that he was hungry, and wondering mildly where he was, he got up.

As soon as he appeared on deck another mad white man fell upon him.

"Ah wants to go to Af'ica, cap'n," he protested, "when I holp dem niggers loadin' yestiddy Ah thought us was all goin' on dis boat."

The white man bore him down with tides of profanity. "God in heaven, you niggers will drive me crazy. Don't you know where this boat is going? It's going to Natchez."

"Dat suit me all right, jes' so she pass Af'ica. You jes' tell me when we gits dar and if she don't stop I kin jump off and swim to de bank."

The man looked at him for a long minute quite in amazement.

"En don't worry about de fare neither, suh," his passenger hastened to reassure him. "I got money: I kin pay it."

"How much you got?"

"Plenty, cap'n," he replied grandly, digging in his overalls. His outthrust hand held four silver dollars, and some smaller coins. The white man took the four dollars.

"Well, I'll take you as far as Africa for this. And you get on up there and help them niggers shift cargo until we get there."

"Yas suh!" he said with alacrity. He paused again. "But you'll sho' tell me at de right station, won't you, cap'n?"

"Yeh, sure. But beat it now, and help them other boys. G'on, now."

He helped the other boys while they passed under the perfect day from one shimmering reach of the river to another; and again the sun hung redly in the west. Bells rang somewhere and the boat sheered in toward the shore. More bells, the boat lost speed and nosed easily into the mud beneath a row of barrels. The white cap'n, the mad one, leaned down from the front porch above his head.

"All right, Jack," he roared, "here you are. Help put them barrels on board, and Africa is about a mile across them fields yonder."

He stood to watch the boat draw away from the shore, trailing black smoke from its tall funnels across the evening; then he shouldered his gun and struck inland. He had not gone far when he thought of the lions and bears he would probably meet, so he stopped and loaded his gun.

After walking until all the light was gone and the Dipper swung majestically down the west, he knew that he must be well into Africa, and that it was time to eat and sleep again. To eat he could not, so he decided to find a safe place to sleep. Tomorrow he could probably kill a rabbit. He suddenly found a fence beside him; across it loomed something that might be a haystack. He climbed the fence and something rose horribly from almost under his feet.

He knew stark and terrible fear. His gun leaped to his shoulder and roared and flamed in the darkness, and the lion or whatever it was plunged bellowing away into the night. He could feel sweat cold as copper pieces on his face and he ran toward the haystack and clawed madly at it, trying to climb it. His fear grew with his futile efforts, then cooled away, allowing him to mount the slippery thing. Once on top he felt safe, but he was cautious to place the shotgun close to his hand as he lay on his belly staring into the night. The thing he had shot was quiet now, but the night was filled with sound.

A light came twinkling along the ground and soon he could see legs criss-crossing it, and he heard voices in a language he could not understand. Savages, he thought, folks that eat you; and he crouched lower in his straw. The light and the voices passed on in the direction the beast he had shot had taken; soon the light stopped beside a blotched thing that swelled up from the ground, and the voices rose in imprecation.

"Gentlemen!" he breathed. "I mus' a shot dem folks' own private lion."

But a lion was a lion. And so he lay hidden while the light moved on away and was lost at last, and the stars swung over him, and he slept.

He was shaken into wakefulness. He threw an arm across his eyes. That strange language was in his ears again and he opened his eyes to see a small dark-skinned man kneeling over him with a pistol. The language he could not understand, but the language the pistol talked he could.

They are going to eat me! he thought. His leg gathered and sickled, the man toppled backward toward the ground, and as an animal leaps he flung himself bodily earthward. A pistol went off and something slapped him dully high in the shoulder. He replied, and a man flopped to the ground. He leaped to his feet and ran, while bullets whined past him. The fence was before him: he turned to follow it, seeking a gate.

His left arm was warm and wet, and there at the turn of the fence was a gate. The shooting behind him continued, he clutched his own gun as he saw a running figure, trying to cut him off at the gate. As they drew together he saw that this one was a member of his own race. "Out de way, nigger," he gasped at the other's waving arms; and he saw the expression of ludicrous amazement on the man's face as his gun crashed again.

His breath came in gulping lungsful. He must stop. Here was a ditch, and a long embankment. Just ahead, where another embankment intersected it, was a small copse. Into this he plunged, concealed, and lay on his back, panting. His heaving lungs at last breathed easier. Then he discovered the wound in his shoulder. He looked at his blood in surprise. "Now when you suppose dat happen?" he thought. "Whew! Dese Af'ikins shoots niggers jes' like white folks does."

He bound it crudely, then took stock of the situation. He had shelter, and that was all. There were still eighteen shells left. And he would need them: there was already one man about two hundred yards away, holding a rifle and watching his thicket. "Don't act like he gwine bother me right soon," he decided. "I'll jes' rest here twell dark, and den I'm gwine back to Mist' Bob. Af'ica sho' ain't no place fer civilized folks—steppin' on lions, and bein' shot, and havin' to shoot folks yo'self. But I guess dese Af'icans is used to it."

His shoulder began to throb dully. He twisted and turned in his mounting fever. How thirsty he was! He had been hungry, but now he was only thirsty, and he thought of the cool brown creek at home, and the cold spring in the wood lot. He raised his sweating face, and saw the watchman had drawn closer in. He raised his gun, aiming the best he could with one hand, and fired. The watchman fell backward, leaped to his feet and ran dodging beyond range. "Jes' to skeer you," he muttered.

Things were beginning to look funny, and his shoulder

hurt dreadfully. He dozed a moment and thought he was at home again; he waked to pain and dozed again. Dozing and waking, he passed the long day, crawling at intervals to sip the muddy, stinking water in the ditch. At last he waked to night, and lanterns and fires, and men walking in the firelight and talking.

He had dragged himself down the bank for water, and as he returned an automobile's lights were suddenly turned full on him. A voice screamed, and bullets whipped about him. He plunged back to his copse and fired blindly at the lights. A man shrieked and bullets ripped and tore at the thicket: the limbs were whipped as by a gale, tortured against the sky. He was seared as with hot irons, and he lowered his head, pressing his face into the muddy earth.

The firing suddenly ceased; the silence literally dragged him from the regions of oblivion. He thrust his gun forward, waiting. At last the darkness detached itself and became two things; and in the flash of his point-blank explosion he saw two men crouching. One of them fired a pistol almost in his face, and fled.

Again it was dawn. The sun rose, became hot, and marched above his head. He was at home, working in the fields; he was asleep, fighting his way from out a nightmare; he was a child again—no, he was a bird, a big one like a buzzard, drawing endless black circles on a blue sky.

Again the sun sank. The west was like blood: it was his own blood painted onto a wall. Supper in the pot, and night where there were no fires and people moving around them, and then all stopping as though they were waiting for something to happen.

He raised his face from the mud and looked at the circle of fires about him. It looked as though everybody had gathered at one place, directly in front of him, all watching or waiting for something. Let them wait: to-morrow he'll be at home, with Mr. Bob to curse him in his gentle voice, and regular folks to work and laugh and talk with.

Here was a wind coming up: the branches and bushes about him whipped suddenly to a gale fiercer than any yet; flattened and screamed, and melted away under it. And he, too, was a tree caught in that same wind: he felt the dull blows of it, and the rivening of himself into tattered and broken leaves.

The gale died away, and all broken things were still. His black, kind, dull, once-cheerful face was turned up to the sky and the cold, cold stars. Africa or Louisiana: what care they?

The Kid Learns

————◆————

COMPETITION is everywhere: competition makes the world go round. Not love, as some say. Who would want a woman nobody else wanted? Not me. And not you. And not Johnny. Same way about money. If nobody wanted the stuff, it wouldn't be worth fighting for. But more than this is being good in your own line, whether it is selling aluminum or ladies' underwear or running whiskey, or what. Be good, or die.

"Listen," said Johnny, tilted back against the wall in his chair, "a man ain't only good in our business because he'd get his otherwise, he's good because he wants to be a little better than the best, see?"

"Sure," said his friend Otto, sitting beside him, not moving.

"Anybody can keep from getting bumped off. All you gotta do is get took on a street gang or as a soda squirt. What counts is being good as you can—being good as any of 'em. Getting yours or not getting yours just shows how good you are or how good you ought to of been."

"Sure," agreed his friend Otto, tilting forward his brief derby and spitting.

"Listen, I ain't got nothing against the Wop, see; but he sets hisself up as being good and I sets myself up as being good, and some day we got to prove between us which is the best."

"Yeh," said Otto, rolling a slender cigarette and flicking a match on his thumb nail, "but take your time. You're young, see; and he's an old head at this. Take your time. Get some age onto you and I'm playing you on the nose at any odds. They wasn't no one ever done a better job in town than the way you taken that stuff away from him last week, but get some age onto you before you brace him, see? I'm for you: you know damn well."

"Sure," said Johnny in his turn, "I ain't no fool. Gimme five years, though, and it'll be Johnny Gray, with not even the bulls to remember the Wop. Five years, see?"

"That's the kid. They ain't nothing to complain, the way we done lately. Let her ride as she lays, and when the time comes we'll clean 'em all."

"And he's right," thought Johnny, walking down the street. "Take time, and get yourself good. They ain't nobody good from the jump: you got to learn to be good. I ain't no fool, I got sense enough to lay off the Wop until the time comes. And when it does—goodnight."

He looked up and his entrails became briefly cold—not with fear, but with the passionate knowledge of what was some day to be. Here was the Wop in an identical belted coat and Johnny felt a sharp envy in spite of himself. They passed; Johnny nodded, but the other only jerked a casual, patronizing finger at him. Too proud to look back, he could see in his mind the swagger of the other's revealed shoulders and the suggestion of a bulge over his hip. Some day! Johnny swore beneath his breath, and he ached for that day.

Then he saw her.

Down the street she came, swinging her flat young body with all the awkward grace of youth, swinging her thin young arms; beneath her hat he saw hair neither brown nor gold, and gray eyes. Clean as a colt she swung past him, and turning to follow her with his eyes and all the vague longing of his own youth, he saw the Wop step gracefully out and accost her.

Saw her recoil, and saw the Wop put his hand on her arm. And Johnny knew that that thing he had wanted to wait for until his goodness was better had already come. The Wop had prisoned both her arms when he thrust between them, but he released his grasp in sheer surprise on recognizing Johnny.

"Beat it," commanded Johnny coldly.

"Why, you poor fish, whatayou mean? You talking to me?"

"Beat it, I said," Johnny repeated.

"You little —— —— ——," and the older man's eyes grew suddenly red, like a rat's. "Don't you know who I am?" He thrust Johnny suddenly aside and again grasped the girl's arm. The back of her hand was pressed against her mouth and she was immovable with fear. When he touched her she screamed, Johnny leaped and struck the Wop on his unguarded jaw, and she fled down the street, wailing. Johnny's pistol was out and he stood over the felled man as Otto ran up.

"My God!" Otto shouted, "you've done it now!" He

dragged a weighted bit of leather from his pocket. "I don't dast croak him here. I'll put him out good, and you beat it, get out of town, quick!" He tapped the still groggy man lightly and ran. "Beat it quick, for God's sake!" he cried over his shoulder. But Johnny had already gone after the girl, and a policeman, running heavily, appeared.

Before a darkened alleyway he overtook her. She had stopped, leaning against the wall with her face in the crook of her arm, gasping and crying. When he touched her she screamed again, whirling and falling. He caught and supported her.

"It ain't him, it's me," he told her obscurely. "There, there; it's all right. I laid him out."

She clung to him, sobbing; and poor Johnny gazed about him, trapped. Cheest, what did you do with a weeping girl?

"Now, now, baby," he repeated, patting her back awkwardly, as you would a dog's, "it's all right. He won't bother you. Tell me where you live, and I'll take you home."

"O-o-o-oh, he sc-scared me s-o," she wailed, clinging to him. Poor kid, she didn't know that he was the one to be scared, that his was the life that was about to take a dark and unknown corner, for better or worse, only the gods knew. There is still time to get out of town, though, caution told him. Otto is right; he knows best. Leave her and beat it, you fool! Leave her, and him back yonder? Youth replied. Not by your grandmother's false teeth, I won't.

He felt her pliant young body shudder with fear and her choked weeping.

"There, there, kid," he repeated inanely. He didn't know what to say to 'em, even. But he must get her away from here. The Wop would be about recovering now, and he'd be looking for him. He held her closer and her trembling gradually died away; and looking about him he almost shouted with relief. Here was old Ryan the cop's house, that had known him boy and lad for fifteen years. The very place.

"Why, say, here's the very place. Mrs. Ryan knows me, she'll look after you until I come back for you."

She clasped him sharply in her thin arms. "No, no, don't leave me! I'm so scared!"

"Why, just for a minute, honey," he reassured her, "just until I find where he went, see? We don't wanta stumble on him again."

"No, no, no, he'll hurt you!" Her wet salty face was against his. "You mustn't! You mustn't!"

"Sure, just a while, baby. I won't be no time." She moaned against Johnny's face and he kissed her cold mouth, and it was as though dawn had come among the trees where the birds were singing. They looked at each other a moment.

"Must you?" she said in a changed voice, and she allowed herself to be led to the dark door; and they clung to each other until footsteps came along the passage within the house. She put her arms around Johnny's neck again.

"Hurry back," she whispered, "and oh, be careful. I'm so afraid!"

"Baby!"

"Sweetheart!"

The door opened upon Mrs. Ryan, there was a brief

explanation, and with her damp kiss yet on his face, Johnny ducked quickly from the alleyway.

Here were flying remote stars above, but below were flashing lights and paved streets, and all the city smells that he loved. He could go away for a while, and then come back, and things—lights and streets and smells— would be the same. "No!" he swore. "I've got a girl now. I ruther be bumped off than have her know I run." But ah, if this could have been put off a while! How sweet she is! Is this love, I wonder? he thought, or is it being afraid, makes me want to run back to her and risk letting things work themselves out instead of doing it myself? Anyway, I done it for her: I wasn't double-crossing the boys. I had to do it: anyone can see that.

"Well, I ain't as good as I wanted, but I can be as good as I can." He looked again at the flying stars, his pistol loose in his pocket, and smelled again the smells of food and gasoline that he loved; and one stepped quickly from out a doorway.

Why, say, here she was again beside him, with her young body all shining and her hair that wasn't brown and wasn't gold and her eyes the color of sleep; but she was somehow different at the same time.

"Mary?" said Johnny, tentatively.

"Little sister Death," corrected the shining one, taking his hand.

The Liar

———◆———

Four men sat comfortably on the porch of Gibson's store, facing the railroad tracks and two nondescript yellow buildings. The two buildings belonged to the railroad company, hence they were tidy in an impersonal way, and were painted the same prodigious yellow. The store, not belonging to the railroad company, was not painted. It squatted stolidly against a rising hill, so that the proprietor could sit at ease, spitting into the valley, and watch the smoke-heralded passing of casual trains. The store and the proprietor resembled each other, slovenly and comfortable; and it was seldom that the owner's was the only chair tilted against the wall, and his the only shavings littering the floor.

Today he had four guests. Two of these had ridden in from the hills for trivial necessities, the other two had descended from the morning's local freight; and they sat in easy amity, watching the smoke from the locomotive dwindle away down the valley.

"Who's that feller, coming up from the deepo?" spoke one at last. The others followed his gaze and the stranger mounted the path from the station under their steady provincial stare. He was roughly dressed—a battered felt hat, a coarse blue cloth jacket and corduroy trousers—a costume identical with that of at least one of the watchers.

"Never seen him before. He don't live hereabouts, that I know of," murmured the proprietor. "Any of you boys know him?"

They shook their heads. "Might be one of them hill fellers. They stays back yonder all the year round, some of 'em ain't never been out." The speaker, a smallish man with a large round bald head and a long saturnine face in which his two bleached eyes were innocent and keen—like a depraved priest—continued: "Feller over to Mitchell says one of 'em brung his whole family into town one day last month to let 'em see a train. Train blowed, and his wife and six-seven children started milling round kind of nervous; but when she come in sight around the bend the whole bunch broke for the woods.

"Old man Mitchell himself had drove down fer his paper, and them hill folks run right spang over his outfit: tore his buggy all to pieces and scart his hoss so bad it took 'em till next day noon to catch him. Yes, sir, heard 'em whooping and hollering all night, trying to head that hoss into something with a fence around it. They say he run right through old Mis' Harmon's house—" The narrator broke down over his own invention. His audience laughed too, enjoying the humor, but tolerantly, as one laughs at a child. His fabling was well known. And though like all peoples who live close to the soil, they were by nature veracious, they condoned his unlimited imagination for the sake of the humor he achieved and which they understood.

The laughter ceased, for the newcomer was near. He

mounted the shaky steps and stood among them, a dark-favored man. "Morning, gentlemen," he greeted them without enthusiasm.

The proprietor, as host, returned his greeting. The others muttered something, anything, as was the custom. The stranger entered the store and the owner rose reluctantly and luxuriously to follow him.

"Say," spoke the raconteur, "ever notice how spry Will is for trade? See him jump up when a customer comes in, and nigh tromps his heels off herding him inside? Minds me of the time—"

"Shet up, Ek," another told him equably. "You already told one lie this morning. Give a man time to smoke a pipe betwixt 'em, leastways. Mebbe that stranger'd like to hear ye. And Will'd hate to miss it, too." The others guffawed, and spat.

Gibson and his customer returned; the proprietor sank with a sigh into his chair and the other, bearing a piece of cheese and a paper sack of crackers, lowered himself onto the top step, his back against a post, partly facing them. He began his meal while they stared at him, gravely and without offense, as children, and all whose desires and satisfactions are simple, can.

"Say, Will," said one after a while, "you come near missing one of Ek's yarns. Us fellers stopped him, though. Now, Ek, you kin go ahead."

"Lissen," said the one called Ek, readily, "all you boys think that ever' time I open my mouth it's to do a little blanket stretching, but lemme tell you something cur'ous that reely happened. 'Twas like this—"

He was interrupted. "Il'y, Will, git out yer hoss medicine: Ek's took sick."

"Musta had a stroke. We kept telling him ter stay outen them sunny fields."

"Yes, sir; shows what work'll do fer you."

"No, boys, it's that licker them Simpson boys makes: Makes a man tell the truth all the time. Sho' better keep it outen the courts, or ever'body'll be in jail."

Ek had vainly striven to surmount the merriment. "You fellers don't know nothing," he roared. "Feller comes trying to tell you the truth—" They shouted him down again, and Will Gibson summed the matter up.

"Why, Ek, we ain't doubting your ability to tell the truth when it's necessary, like in court or meeting house; but they ain't no truth ever happened as entertaining as your natural talk, hey boys? He's better'n a piece in the theayter, ain't he, fellers?"

The others assented loudly, but Ek refused to be mollified. He sat in offended dignity. The others chuckled at intervals, but at last the merriment was gone and there was no sound save the stranger's methodical crunching. He, seemingly, had taken no part in the laughter. Far up the valley a train whistled; echo took the sound and toyed with it, then let it fade back into silence.

But silence was unbearable to Ek. At last it overcame his outraged dignity. "Say," he went easily into narrative, "lemme tell you something cur'ous that reely happened to me yest'day. I was over to Mitchell yest'day waiting for the early local, when I meets up with Ken Rogers, the sheriff. We passed the time of day and he says to me, what am I doing today, and I tells him I aim to ride No. 12 over home. Then he says he's looking for somebody like me, asking me wasn't I raised in the hills. I tells him I was, and how when I turned twenty-one, paw decided I had ought to wear shoes. I hadn't never worn no shoes, and was young and skittish as a colt in them days.

"Well, sir, you may believe it or not, but when they come to my pallet that morning with them new shoes, I up and lit out of there in my shirt tail and took to the woods. Paw sent word around to the neighbors and they organized a hunt same as a bear hunt, with axes and ropes and dogs. No guns, though; paw held that to shoot me would be a waste of manpower, as I could stand up to a day's work with any of 'em.

"Well, sir, it took 'em two days to git me, and they only got me then when them big man-eating hounds of Lem Haley's put me up a tree in Big Sandy bottom, twenty miles from home. And mebbe you won't believe it, but it took paw and three strong men to put them shoes on me." He led the laughter himself, which the stranger joined. "Yes, sir; them was the days. But lemme see, I kind of got off the track. Where was I? Oh, yes. Well, the sheriff he says to me can't I go back in the hills a ways with him. And I says, well, I dunno; I got some business in Sidon to tend to today—"

"Same business you're tending to now, I reckon?" interrupted one of his audience. "Got to git back where folks believe him when he says he's telling the truth."

"Now, look-a-here," began the affronted narrator, when the proprietor interfered. "Hush up, you Lafe; let him finish his tale. G'on, Ek, won't nobody bother you again."

Ek looked at him in gratitude and resumed. "Well, listen. The sheriff, he says to me, he needs a man that knows them hill folks to go in with him. Been some trouble of some kind and he wants to clear it up. But them hill people is so leary that they's liable to shoot first, before a man kin state his point. So he wants I should go along with him and kind of mollify 'em, you might say, promising to get me back in time to catch the evening train. Well, they ain't nothing I couldn't put off a day or so, so I goes with him. He's got his car all ready and a deppity waiting, so we piles in and lit out.

"It was as putty a day as I ever see and we was having a good time, laughing and talking back and forth—"

Lafe interrupted again: "Must of been, with a set of fellers't never heard your lies before."

"Be quiet, Lafe," Gibson commanded peremptorily.

"—and first thing I knew, we come to a place where the road played out altogether. 'Have to walk from here on,' sheriff says, so we runs the car off the road a ways, and struck out afoot. Well, sir, I was born and raised in them hills, but I never seen that stretch where we was before—all ridges, and gullies where you could sling a hoss off and lose him. Finally the sheriff says to me: 'Ek,' he says, 'place we're heading for is jest across that ridge. You go on over to the house, and tell Mrs. Starnes who you are; and Tim and me'll go around yonder way. Probably catch Joe in his lower field. We'll meet you at the house. Might ask Mis' Starnes if she kin git us a little snack ready.'

" 'All right, sheriff,' I says, 'but I don't know nobody through here.'

" 'That's all right,' sheriff says, 'jest go up to the house and tell her me and Joe and Tim'll be 'long soon.' And him and Tim started on around the ridge, and I took the route he give me. Well, sir, I moseyed on up to the top of the ridge, and sho' 'nough, there was a house and a barn setting in the next valley. It didn't look like much of a farm and I just decided them Starneses was average shif'less hill folks. There was a lot of rocks on the ridge where I was, and just as I was thinking what a good place for snakes it was and starting on down to'rds the house— bzzzrrr! went something right behind me. Gentlemen, I jumped twenty foot and lit grabbing rocks. When I had throwed a couple the rattler was gone into a hole; and then I seen three others laying with their heads mashed, and I knowed I must of stumbled into a regular den of 'em. They hadn't been dead long, and from the sample I'd had I knowed how mad the others must be, so I lit a shuck out of there. But I wasn't far from the feller had killed them three, but just how close I never learnt till later.

"I dropped on down through the brush, coming to the house from behind. Down the hill from the barn and between me and the house was a spring in a rocky gully. The spring was railed off from cattle. There was gullies and rocks ever'where: I never seen such pore, rocky land—sink holes full of rocks and narrer as wells. I had to jump 'em like a goat.

"I was about half-way down the hill when I seen a feller moving down at the spring. I hadn't seen him before. He jest wasn't there when I looked once, but there he was when I looked again, rising up by the spring. He had a wooden box under his arm. I never knowed where he come from.

"Knowing how skittish them hill folks are, I was jest about to sing out when he put his finger in his mouth and whistled. I thought mebbe he was calling his dog, and I was thinking to myself it was a sorry dog that never suspicioned me when I was this close, when a woman come to the back door of the house. She stood there a minute, shading her eyes and looking all around at the ridges, but she never did look to'rds the spring. Then she stepped out, toting something in her hand, and started fer the spring on the run. Then I could see she had her Sunday hat on, and that the thing in her hand was a carpetbag. Fellers, she jest flew down that hill.

" 'Uh, uh,' thinks I to myself, 'they's something going on here that I don't know about, and that Starnes don't know nothing about, neither.' The sheriff seemed mighty certain he wouldn't be to home, and I never seen a man and wife go to all that trouble to go anywheres.

"Well, sir, they met at the spring. The feller had set his little box down careful, and they was clamped together like two sheep in a storm, and was a-kissing. 'Uh, uh!' thinks I, 'here's something else me and Starnes don't know nothing about, and what'd make him itch if he did.' I was higher up than them two, and I taken a look around fer sheriff and Tim, and I seen a lone feller coming down the valley. They couldn't see him a tall, but jest when I seen him, he spied them. He stopped a minute like he was studying, then he come on, not hiding exactly, but walking careful.

"Meanwhile, them two at the spring was bent over the feller's little box, and I seen her jump back and kind of squeal. Well, sir, things was getting cur'ouser and cur'ouser ever' minute, and I was a-wishing and a-griping for sheriff and Tim to git there. 'If sheriff's wanting something to clear up,' I thinks to myself, 'I got it here waiting fer him.' And about then things begun to pop.

"Them two at the spring looked up all on a sudden.

They had either seen or heard the other feller; so he walked in bold as you please. The woman she kind of comes behind the first feller; then she drops her bag and makes a bee-line fer the other one, the feller that jest come up, and tries to grab him round the neck. He flings her off and she fell flat, but jumped up and tried to grab him again.

"Well, sir, she kep' on trying to hold his arm and he kep' on a-flinging her off, all the time walking not fast but steady to'rds number one. Finally she sees she can't stop 'em, so she backed off with her hands kind of against her side, and I can see she is scared most to death. Them two fellers is about a yard apart, when number two hauled off and knocked the other one clean into the spring. He jumped up right away and grabbed up a rail from the fence that kep' cattle out of the spring. The woman hollered and grabbed at number two again, and while he was shaking her loose, number one ups and hits him over the head with his rail, and he dropped like a ox. Them hill folks has got hard heads, but it seemed to me I could hear that feller's skull bust. Leastways, he never moved again. The woman backed off, clamping her head betwixt her hands; and the feller watched him awhile, then throwed away his rail.

"Well, sir, you could of knocked me down with a straw. There I was, watching murder, skeered to move, and no sign of sheriff and Tim. I've got along fine without no law officers, but I sho' needed one then." Ek stopped, with consummate art, and gazed about on his hearers. Their eyes were enraptured on his face, the hot black gaze of the stranger seemed like a blade spitting him against the wall, like a pinned moth. The train whistled again, unheard.

"Go on, go on," breathed Gibson.

He drew his gaze from the stranger's by an effort of will, and found that the pleasant May morning was suddenly chill. For some reason he did not want to continue.

"Well, sir, I didn't know whether the feller would finish his job right then or not; seemed like he didn't know himself. And all the time the woman was like she was took by a spell. Finally he walked over and picked the unconscious feller up, and carried him about fifteen foot down the gully, then dumped him like a sack of meal into one of them narrow sink holes. And all the time the woman was watching him like she was turned to stone." The train whistled again and the locomotive came in sight, but not one turned his eyes from the narrator's face.

"Seemed like he had decided what to do now. He run back to'rds where the woman was, and I thinks, my God, he's going to kill her, too. But no, he's just after his box. He grabs it up and come back to where he had throwed the other feller. Well, sir, if I could have been cur'ous over anything right then, I would have been cur'ous over what he was a-doing now. But as it was, I was past thinking: jest goggle-eyed, like a fish when you jerk him out the water.

"And all the time this feller is fiddling with his box, standing on the edge of that sink hole. All on a sudden he helt it out from him, shaking it over the hole. Finally something all knotted and shiny like a big watch chain fell out of it and dropped, shining and twisting, into the place where the other feller was.

"Then I knowed who'd killed them rattlers."

"My God," said someone.

"Yes, sir. They'd planned to fix that there snake where number two'd stumble on it when he come in, only he come too soon for 'em."

"My God!" repeated the voice, then the one called Lafe screamed:

"Look out!"

A pistol said whow, the sound slammed against the front of the store and roared across the porch. Ek rolled from his chair and thumped on the floor, tried to rise, and fell again. Lafe sprang erect, but the others sat in reft and silent amaze, watching the stranger leaping down the path toward the track and the passing train; saw him recklessly grasp a car ladder and, shaving death by inches, scramble aboard.

* * *

Later, when the doctor had ridden ten miles, dressed Ek's shoulder, cursed him for a fool, and gone, the four of them took him to task.

"Well, Ek, I guess you learnt your lesson. You'll know better than tell the truth again."

"Ain't it the beatingest thing? Here's a man lied his way through life fer forty years and never got a scratch, then sets out to tell the truth fer once in his life, and gets shot."

"But what was your point," Will Gibson reiterated, "in telling your fool yarn right in front of the feller that did it? Didn't you know him again?"

Ek turned his fever exasperated face to them. "I tell

you that it was all a lie, ever last word of it. I wasn't nowhere near Mitchell yest'day."

They shook their heads at his obstinacy; then Gibson, seeing that they were increasing the patient's fever, drove them out. The last to go, he turned at the door for a parting shot.

"I don't know whether you were lying, or were telling the truth, but either way, you must get a whole lot of satisfaction out of this. If you were lying, you ought to be shot for telling one so prob'le that it reely happened somewhere; and if you were telling the truth, you ought to be shot for having no better sense than to blab it out in front of the man that done the killing. Either way, if you ain't learnt a lesson, I have. And that is, don't talk at all lessen you have to, and when you got to talk, tell the truth."

"Aw, get out of here," snarled Ek. And convicted of both truthfulness and stupidity, he turned his face bitterly to the wall, knowing that his veracity as a liar was gone forever.

Episode

———◆———

EVERY DAY at noon they pass. He in a brushed
suit and a gray hat, never collarless nor tieless, she in a
neat cotton print dress and a sunbonnet. I have seen her
any number of times, sitting and rocking upon wooden
porches before the crude, shabby cottages among my
own hills in Mississippi.

They are at least sixty. He is blind and his gait is
halting and brittle. Talking in a steady stream, gesturing
with her knotty hand, she leads him daily to the cathedral
to beg; at sunset she returns for him and takes him home.
I had not seen her face until Spratling from the balcony
called to her. She looked to both sides and then behind
her without discovering us. At Spratling's second call she
looked up.

Her face is brown, and timeless and merry as a gnome's
and toothless: her nose and chin know each other.

"Are you in a hurry?" he asked.

"Why?" she replied brightly.

"I'd like to sketch you."

She watched his face keenly, not comprehending.

"I'd like to make a picture of you," he explained.

"Come down," she replied promptly, smiling. She spoke to the man with her and he obediently tried to sit down upon the narrow concrete base of the garden fence. He fell heavily and a passer-by helped her raise him to his feet. I left Spratling feverishly seeking a pencil and descended with a chair for him, and I saw that she was actually trembling—not with age, but with pleased vanity.

"Assiz, Joe," she ordered, and he sat down, his sightless face filled with that remote godlike calm known only to the blind. Spratling with his sketch pad appeared. She took her place beside the seated man with her hand on his shoulder: one knew immediately that they had been photographed so on their wedding day.

She was a bride again; with that ability for fine fabling which death alone can rob us of, she was once more dressed in silk (or its equivalent) and jewels, a wreath and a veil, and probably a bouquet. She was a bride again, young and fair, with her trembling hand on young Joe's shoulder; Joe beside her was once more something to shake her heart with dread and adoration and vanity—something to be a little frightened of.

A casual passer-by felt it and stopped to look at them. Even blind Joe felt it through her hand on his shoulder. Her dream clothed him, too, in youth and pride; he too assumed that fixed and impossible attitude of the male and his bride being photographed in the year 1880.

"No, no," Spratling told her, "not like that." Her face fell. "Turn toward him, look at him," he added quickly.

She obeyed, still facing us.

"Turn your head too; look at him."

"But you can't see my face then," she objected.

"Yes, I can. Besides, I'll draw your face later."

Appeased, her smile broke her face into a million tiny wrinkles, like an etching, and she took the position he wanted.

At once she became maternal. She was no longer a bride; she had been married long enough to know that Joe was not anything to be either loved or feared very passionately, but on the contrary he was something to be a little disparaging of; that after all he was only a large, blundering child. (You knew she had borne children by now—perhaps lost one.) But he was hers and another would be as bad probably, so she would make the best of it, remembering other days.

And Joe, again taking her mood through her hand on his shoulder, was no longer the dominating male. And he too, remembering other days when he had come to her for comfort, took her new dream. His arrogance dissolved from him and he sat quiet under her touch, helpless yet needing no help, sightless and calm as a god who has seen both life and death and found nothing of particular importance in either of them.

Spratling finished.

"Now the face," she reminded him quickly. And now there was something in her face that was not her face. It partook of something in time, in the race, ambiguous, enigmatic. Was she posing? I wondered, watching her. She was facing Spratling, but I don't believe her eyes saw him, nor the wall behind him. Her eyes were contemplative, yet personal—it was as if someone had whispered a sublime and colossal joke in the ear of an idol.

Spratling finished, and her face became the face of a

woman of sixty, toothless and merry as a gnome's. She came over to see the sketch, taking it in her hands.

"Got any money?" Spratling asked me.

I had fifteen cents. She returned the picture without comment and took the coins.

"Thank you," she said. She touched her husband and he rose. "Thank you for the chair," she nodded and smiled at me, and I watched them move slowly down the alley, wondering what I had seen in her face—or had I seen anything at all. I turned to Spratling. "Let's see it."

He was staring at the sketch. "Hell," he said. I looked at it. And then I knew what I had seen in her face. The full-face sketch had exactly the same expression as the Mona Lisa.

Ah, women, who have but one eternal age! And that is no age.

Country Mice

———◆———

M Y FRIEND the bootlegger's motor car is as long as a steamboat and the color of a chocolate ice cream soda. It is trimmed with silver from stem to stern like an expensive lavatory. It is upholstered in maroon leather and attached to it, for emergencies and convenience, is every object which the ingenuity of its maker could imagine my friend ever having any possible desire for or need of. Except a coffin. It is my firm belief that on the first opportunity his motor car is going to retaliate by quite viciously obliterating him.

We were pursuing a custom of ours, an obnoxious habit which he had formed for me and which he called "airing off"; i.e., to take the shortest way out of town and then to go somewhere, anywhere, at between forty and seventy miles an hour. He never drives faster than seventy because for some reason his car will not go any faster than seventy miles an hour. I am constantly uneasy over the expectation that some day someone will show him how to make it go eighty miles an hour. And I simply cannot afford an untimely dissolution: I have my living to earn. However, I am by nature an incurable optimist; he seems to enjoy my company, and some day I hope to get a story out of him, for marvelous are the tales he so casually tells me of his early struggles trying to make label and bottle meet. And there you are.

My friend the bootlegger is consistently paradoxical. His shirt is of silk and striped viciously, and collarless; in its front is a ruby stud (genuine) the size of a small olive; looping from his belt to his pocket is a gold and platinum and yet virgin watch chain: he believes it is unlucky to carry a watch, and besides when he goes anywhere he travels by a speed indicator; he owns a gold and elegant cigarette case of fourteen net ounces displacement which, when opened, reveals a brand of cigarettes which may be purchased anywhere at fifty for twenty-five cents. But to get on.

We were, as I think I stated before, airing off. The road was straight and white as a swift unrolling ribbon, and Louisiana rushed by us in a fretful, indistinguishable green. Wind plopped at my ears and my eyelashes turned backward irritatingly, keeping me blinking. Then something happened. I noticed with surprise that the wind no longer plopped so loudly at my ears. Imagine my surprise to find that we were going only thirty-five miles an hour—practically crawling. We were approaching a small village: two rows of houses facing each other across the road.

"They'll have time to dodge after they hear you, at this speed," I shouted warningly at his ear.

"Dodge, hell," he replied. "I'm the one that's dodging." He caught my glance of inquiry and added: "Constable."

"Why, you don't mind a little thing like a hick constable, do you?" I asked in surprise. We had left the village in our dust and the speedometer began to climb.

"Lemme tell you something, brother—" he mashed his gleaming yellow shoe heavily on the throttle "—say what you want to about country cops, call 'em hicks if you want; but when you fool with one of them birds, get up early in the morning to do it, see? I know 'em. I used to think about 'em like you do, but one learned me better." He glanced at the speedometer and mashed his foot harder. She was only doing sixty-six.

"Yes?" I screamed. He stared ahead frowningly, preoccupied. His car was practically new, but I knew that he already dreamed of a car that would go seventy-five miles an hour, or even eighty. It was not seventy miles an hour he wanted, it was five miles an hour for which he pined. But such is the immortal soul of man.

At last she showed seventy and he sighed, settling down to enjoy himself. "Yes sir. You can say what you. . . . 'member when. . . . what you call a hick cop. . . ." The wind tore the words from his tongue. I leaned toward him, clutching my hat.

"I can't hear you!" I screamed diffidently. "If you'd slow down a bit. . . ."

He complied, giving me his quick Italian glance. "I couldn't hear you," I explained when we had dropped to conversational speed.

"Oh sure," he agreed with his habitual courtesy. "This come off when I was in New York. Doing a good business, making lots of jack. I was in with the big fellows, see?" He sighed again in retrospection. "Them was good times then, before them politicians ruined the liquor business. But it's shot to hell, now. No more money in it. I work like a nigger to make a living, even, now; while back in them days. . . ." He brooded briefly toward his lost alcoholic Nirvana. "But now when you got to sell it at thirty-six a case. . . . Well," he said philosophically, "they don't nothing last forever, does it? But she was sure a pretty business at one time. I remember—"

"But about this hick cop," I suggested, recalling him.

"Oh yes. Well, it was in the fall of '20 or '21, when the liquor business was so good, when you could stick 'em one-fifty and two hundred a case. Me and my brother was in the East then. And so this bird I knew comes to me and suggests that we bring a bunch of hooch into New Haven, a town up the road from New York, where they was going to have a big football game, and we'd clean up. New Haven is where one of them big colleges is, I forget the name of it—"

"Yale," I suggested.

"I guess so. Anyway, this bird I'm telling you about had been there and he knew how everything stacked up. My brother he went on up to Montreal to get the stuff lined up and ready to go, and me and the other fellow goes up to New Haven. You been to a college town, ain't you?"

I admitted that I had, and he continued:

"It was a funny town, quiet seeming, but plenty of business in my line. We never had no trouble at all getting ourselves set pretty as you'd want. Waiting for word from my brother, see. We had everything fixed for him, all the cops along the route had been fixed all right, and all he had to do was to bring them trucks right on down like he was going to a Sunday school picnic. They wasn't only one thing we had to worry about—hi-jackers. And we'd fixed him up with as pretty a gang of cutthroats as you ever seen for guards. I knew I could depend on him: honest and clever as the day is long. The day they started out he wired me at New Haven, and so we was all set.

"Well, we mixed around in New Haven and got to know some nice people and we was spending a nice week up there, knowing that everything was jake or Gus, that's my brother, would have wired us, when one night they came a long distance telephone for me.

"Yeh, it was Gus. In some jay town, I forget the name of it. They had had a run-in with some hi-jackers and had turned off the route onto another road and—bang. A hayseed cop that hadn't been fixed held 'em up. Wouldn't listen to reason, wouldn't consider nothing. Color blind, too. So Gus put up his bail and put away his roll and beat it to the telephone. Jees, I was mad. If anybody'd been listening in, I'd a got pinched sure. So me and the other bird grabbed a taxi and caught the first train.

"Well sir, we tried everything with that J. P. Showed him some real money, told him they was more—fellow, I talked to that old gray-haired —— —— —— like a brother. But it never moved him no more than one of them New England rocks; say, I'd a stood more chance buying Republican votes in front of Tammany Hall. I didn't know what to do. But this other bird he wouldn't give up. He said you couldn't tell him they wasn't no way of fixing this thing; that this country had got in a hell of a way if they could sew you up like this. Well, I told him to fly at it, that I'd give him ten bucks a case for all of it we moved. And I went to the hotel and set down so I could groan comfortable.

"I'd been there about an hour, I guess, when here

comes my partner. 'Buck up,' he says, slapping me on the back. 'It's all fixed. It's going to cost us twenty-five a case to move it and we got to do it quick.'

" 'Pinch yourself,' I says, 'you're dreaming.'

" 'Dreaming yourself,' he says. 'You better be glad I got out and done something instead of setting here crying into my own vest.'

" 'All right,' I says, 'if you got the dope, spill it.' I still thought he was kidding me, see?

"But he wasn't. He had got next to the deputy that was guarding the barn where the trucks was, and they had agreed on twenty-five a case. That was pretty steep, but then we'd just shove her up a few dollars ourselves—folks don't care what they give for a case of the stuff, when they are celebrating. Only I wanted to be darn sure we wouldn't be held up again. But this deputy had fixed that, even. He knowed a fellow in Boston that had a airplane, see, and he said he knowed we could get it, though we might have to buy it. So I told him to fly at it and get his buddy here by nightfall, as we didn't have but over tomorrow before the football game was pulled off. So he said all right, he'd have him here like he said.

"Well, sure enough that night the deputy brought the airplane fellow around to see us. And they was as like as two peas: they looked exactly alike. Well sir, I look at my partner and I think for Pete's sake, and he looks at me thinking the same thing. And this deputy says, 'This is my twin brother,' like he'd just thought of it. But when we got down to business the airplane fellow was as stubborn as the J. P. had been. I ought to of knowed then, but seems like our luck was against us: we was worse than two children. What do you think he wanted for his airplane? Not to rent it to us: he couldn't see that at all. We must buy it outright or—good-night. And what you guess he wanted? One thousand dollars."

He pronounced the words with vicious unction. Then he became temporarily unprintable, tramping heavily on the throttle. My spine snapped to our speed.

"And what then?" I shrieked. He slowed down.

"What else could we do? They wasn't no other way to get the stuff there on time, and I could see in that deputy's eye that if we turned his brother down, it was all off all around. They had us, see? All we could hope for was to get our money out now. So me and my partner asked 'em to excuse us a moment while we went into the next room and talked it over.

" 'So this is the way you handle these hick officers, huh?' I says to him.

" 'At least it's better'n the way you handle 'em,' he comes back.

" 'I admit that,' I says, 'specially if you base your calculations on what it's going to cost us.'

" 'That ain't neither here nor there,' he says. 'What we've got to do is to get out the best way we can. And that is—' I seen his point right off.

" '—and that is to hi-jack that deputy for that twenty-five a case as soon as we get started.'

"So we matched, to see which one of us went with the stuff and which one stayed to fix that deputy. And I lost. What? Hell, no. I'd rather of walked in the White House and stuck up the president at his own dinner table than ride in that airplane. But I lost.

"Well, we met 'em at the barn where the trucks was. We had sent Gus on to New Haven to get everything lined up, and the deputy had a couple of men there. And we worked like dogs, putting all we could into that airplane. Finally she had as much as the fellow thought she'd carry and we was all set as soon as it got light. I stalled around so the deputy wouldn't have time to hide the jack, then I paid him what we had agreed on, and him and his brother got the airplane motor started and I called Joe off to one side and tried again to make him swap with me. When I'd look at that damn airplane and think about I was going up in it—I was all ready to call it off and let 'em have the stuff. But I got a weak stomach, anyway, specially before breakfast.

" 'Ah, come on,' Joe says. 'You wanna let 'em see you're yellow?'

" 'Let 'em see. I admit I'm yellow.'

" 'Ah, brace up, brace up. Why, I wouldn't be afraid to go with him, if only I didn't have this other thing to see to.'

" 'Hell,' I says, 'I'll see to that. It'll be a pleasure. You go with him.'

"But he wouldn't do it. 'It's bad luck to change your plans,' he gave as his reason.

" 'I've heard your theory of bad luck lots of times,' I says, 'but that's a new one on me.'

"But by then they was calling us. I felt like a kid does when he don't want to do something he knows he's got to, and so he walks slow and does everything he can think of to put it off. But I had to do it, and here was the deputy saying, 'Well, you ought to have a fine trip,' and me thinking, 'Sure, fine trip,' and that other looking like a big beetle. He give me a—what do you call it? Helmet? Helmet and goggles, and they put 'em on me, and so there wasn't nothing to do but climb in. Jees, I wished then I'd never heard of New Haven, that I was a barber or something. So I made to climb in, see, and Joe was pushing me and my stomach felt funny, and I stopped and looked at Joe and I says: 'Take your hands off me. What you want? Wanna help me get killed?' But Joe was a good sort and so when I was in I held out my hand, thinking what a good guy Joe was after all, see, even if I didn't get back safe.

"Then the fellow climbed up where I was and started strapping a big belt around me, and I told him they wasn't no need of that, that I wasn't only not going to try to jump out but that he wasn't even big enough to throw me out. Well, he said he knowed that, that the belt was in case I fell out.

" 'Fell out?' I says.

" 'Sure,' he says, 'she might buck you out like a horse.'

"Men do funny things, don't they? Anyway, I sat there and I thought I was looking at the ground for the last time. I never was much on walking. Then he got into another seat and opened the throttle wide open. I shut my eyes and grabbed something, and I swore I was going to sit like that until we got to New Haven. We hadn't gone far when the engine slowed up again and I opened my eyes right quick and there was a house and a fence right in front of us. I couldn't even shut my eyes again.

"And then just as I thought we was going right into it we slewed around and when I got my breath again we was headed back the way we come. Then he stepped on her again and I shut my eyes and held on. And after a time when it got to what I thought was a smooth place I sneaked another look and I was right opposite the top of a tree and if I'd looked long enough I could of looked right down on top of a couple of houses. And then—but I got a weak stomach, anyways.

"Well, after a while I seen they wasn't nothing to do but stay where I was and make the best of it. And I sure aimed to stay there as long as he did. I didn't dare turn around to see where he was, and looking out made me dizzy, and so there I was. But I learned one thing: I don't overwork my luck no more. Yes sir, ever since then I've been as easy on my luck as I could.

"If you'd ask me how it looked from up there, I couldn't tell you. I don't know. But I looked out to the side once and seen the whole ocean before I could get my eyes shut again. The ground is good enough for me.

"Anyway, after a while it felt like all my insides was falling out of me, and I shut my eyes tighter and held on. And then we bumped on the ground and after a while we stopped. Well sir, I sat in that damn thing for about ten minutes before I could move, and when I did get out it was like I had had a spell of sickness or something. We was in a big field on the edge of town, and the airplane fellow was walking about smoking a cigarette. And I lit one too, and felt a little better. I felt like taking a handful of that dirt and eating it.

"The fellow had run the airplane across the field and up close to a big cliff where you couldn't see it except you were in the field, and pretty soon here came Gus with a couple of trucks. He had been laying for us where the deputy had told him to watch out, and had followed us, see. Well, we set to work and transferred her. There was three or four fellows who come up to see what was going on, and one of 'em says, 'What you got there, mister?' And Gus says right off, 'U. S. mail, brother,' and kept right on.

"Pretty soon we was through and Gus got his boys right on out with the stuff. And I took a full breath for the first time. The airplane fellow was standing around watching us, and he says:

" 'Whatcher going to do with your crate?'

" 'Crate?' I says. He waved his hand at the airplane. 'Hell,' I says, 'I ain't got no airplane. I don't never want to see one again even.'

" 'What'll you take for it?' he says. 'I might buy it back from you.'

" 'Gimme a hundred,' I says, 'and take it.'

"So he did. I was glad to get even that much back, see? All I wanted was to break even, and I figured we'd about do that, even if we never got the rest of our stuff. But I figured on doing that in a couple of days. I was like you: I called 'em hicks myself, then.

"Well, me and Gus held the thing while he started it up, and we watched him go off in it. He turned and waved his arm at us, and I waved back. 'So long,' I thinks, 'and may I never see you again.' That's what I thought then.

"All of a sudden Gus hauls a telegram out of his pocket. 'For you,' he says. 'I nearly forgot it.'

"It was from Joe and it said: 'Hold Gilman, no matter how. Coming next train.'

" 'Gilman?' I says. 'Who's Gilman?'

" 'Oh, that's the name of that J. P. that sewed us up,' Gus tells me.

" 'Hell,' I says, 'how can I hold Gilman here? Joe must be coo-coo. Hold Gilman?'

"Gus couldn't make no more out of it than me, and
so we got in his car and drove on to town. And at the
hotel we found one of the boys waiting in the room with
a couple of bottles. They had got the stuff put away all
o. k. We was all set for Joe to get back now. And then
we opened a bottle."

We had been in town for some time. My friend drove
skillfully while he talked.

"Well?" I prompted.

He laughed harshly. "Well is good," he said. "Do you
know what was in them bottles?" I was silent, and he
answered himself: "Water. Pure unadulterated water; the
stuff that it rains, you know." He became again unprintable. Then he settled down once more to narration.
"And every damn one of them bottles was the same. I
jumped Gus right off, but he swore they was all right
when he bought 'em and they wasn't no chance for anybody to tamper with 'em until they was stopped. He had
opened one or two of 'em on the road.

"And then about dark Joe comes bulging in. Me and
him both says 'How about it?' at the same time.

" 'Did you turn the trick?' I says.

" 'Where's Gilman?' he says quick, not answering me.

" 'What's he got to do with it?' I asks.

" 'Everything,' Joe says, looking like he was about to
have a stroke.

" 'Didn't you get the stuff?' I asks, feeling my insides
turning cold.

" 'How could I? The one that drove you down here
had it all the time. The other one just laughed at me
when I stuck him up. Called me a hick."

" 'You mean to say you ain't got that money?' I says again, trying to understand.

" 'That's exactly what I mean. But if you'll show me where Gilman is I'll damn soon have it.'

" 'Who in hell is Gilman?' I asks. 'You keep on talking about Gilman—'

" 'Didn't you get my wire?' Joe cuts in.

" 'Yeh,' I told him, 'but the only Gilman Gus and me knew was that J. P., that as far as I know is at home eating supper by now.'

" 'And you don't know who Gilman is?' Joe kind of screamed at me. His eyes were popping and his face looked like it would bust right off his shoulders. 'Gilman is the fellow that brought you down here—' " My friend the bootlegger turned a corner viciously. The pedestrian, however, escaped. " 'Him and the deputy are that judge's twin sons!' "

Yo Ho and Two
Bottles of Rum

———◆———

SHE WAS a sweet thing to see, wallowing like a great
enceinte sow in the long swells of the Pacific. Rolling was
her habit: from side to side she went even in the calmest
sea, sighing and groaning like an elephant with an eternal
bellyache, like a huge nondescript dog trying to dislodge
fleas; it was said of her that she rolled even while tied up
to a dock. But in heavy weather, in a sea which gave her
every excuse to wallow to her heart's content, she became
singularly and remarkably steady.

Her best speed was ten knots—four knots from side to
side and six knots forward. Perhaps this was sufficient,
perhaps more speed than this would have blown her crew
overboard. A casual observer would have thought so anyway, looking down from the bridge, seeing them squat-
ting quietly, meager and fleshless, small and naked as
children; yellow wisps of men clothed modestly in shirts,
still and unfathomable as mummies or idols.

Manned by Chinese, officered by the scum of the riff-

raff of the United Kingdom, a scum which even the
catholic stomach of the dominions beyond the seas re-
fuses at intervals, vomiting it over the face of the globe,
she did her six knots, rolling and groaning her stinking
way through Eastern waters from Canton to the Straits,
anywhere the ingenuity of man might send a cargo. She
might be seen anywhere; tied rolling heavily to a wharf
in Singapore, weathering a typhoon in an anchorage
known only to admiralty charts, next year in Bangkok or
the Dutch Indies. Strangely enough her personnel did not
change much. It was as though every soul aboard had
been caught hopelessly in an inescapable dream. A dingy
dream, for she was with the exception of the bridge deck
and the officers' quarters filthy from stem to stern. Her
personality was soiled and kind, she sailed under the
British flag and years ago in Newcastle a humorist with
a clairvoyant eye christened her, when she was youthful
and yet undisillusioned, "Diana."

Pride is a funny thing, in the various forms it takes.
The American or the Latin "goes bad" and drops out of
sight, assimilates himself with people and conditions
among which his destiny casts him, becomes (sentimen-
tally perhaps) noncommittal regarding his nationality.
But the Britisher is still British, the lower he goes the
more blatantly British he becomes. It was so with the
officers of the Diana, particularly with Mr. Freddie
Ayers, the mate. Perhaps the other officers had less to be
British about. The captain was Welsh, his beard was like
a red explosion and he spoke a tongue regarding which
only one thing could be said: It was not English. It was
most palpably not English. The chief engineer was Scot-
tish. He had a face like a bitter walnut and spoke no

tongue whatever. The rest of the officers with the exception of the third mate, who was Eusian [*sic*], and led or was led a dog's life in consequence, being neither one nor the other, yet having a sacred drop or two of British blood to saddle him with the white man's responsibilities while at the same time his lesser strain denied him the white man's pleasures; the rest of them seemed to have sprung blackguards full-fledged from the womb of time, being British and nothing else. The owner's agents seemed to understand the captain, however, and as it was not necessary that anyone understand the chief engineer, they got along just as well. As long as the whisky held out, that is.

Mr. Freddie Ayers did all the talking for them. He talked all the time, waking and sleeping; he slept with his eyes open also, as a matter of precaution, perhaps. It was this, the sight of Mr. Ayers on his back, his china-colored eyes gleaming dully, like a cadaver, that caused the third officer to fear him like death. But waking and in the earlier stages of his daily inebriation Mr. Ayers was the soul of joviality and wit as he sat in the saloon clasping his tumbler, sucking his straight short pipe, so palpably and blatantly British with mackerel eye and his moth-eaten Guardsman's moustache. It was he who prior to killing him through an unavoidable accident dubbed the sibilant flitting messboy "Yo Ho."

"Such a jolly name, y'know," he explained in his insufferable London voice, braying brassily in hearty appreciation at the chief engineer. "Navy fashion, hey?"

The chief gaped his toothless nut-cracker face at the first officer, replying as he did to all questions by sucking a gill of diluted whisky into himself. And Yo Ho the

(123)

messboy became, accepting the name foisted upon him without surprise, appearing on his hissing straw slippers when they bawled for him, receiving their curses, serving them efficiently and with remote yellow tolerance of the vagaries of the white man.

The Diana with a cargo of American-made sewing machines was out of Canton, bound for Bangkok, when Mr. Ayers the mate killed, through an unavoidable accident, Yo Ho the messboy.

The captain stared at Mr. Ayers morosely across the incandescent burst of his beard. "What kill'm for?" he asked.

Mr. Ayers emptied his glass and for the nth time sought to justify himself. "I tell you it was an accident. I mistook him for the bosun. Damned stupid of me, I grant you; but damme, it's done now. I can't recall the blighter, can I, sir?" Mr. Ayers filled his glass again, viciously. "Plenty more of the fellers; one Chinee like another."

The chief engineer here spoke amazingly, supporting the mate. "Do wi'oot," he mumbled. Then quite clearly: "Rrrotten lad." Mr. Ayers and the captain looked at him quickly and he retired modestly into his glass, taking a mouthful, and sat chewing it mildly.

"But what kill'm for?" the captain repeated.

"Dammit, sir," Mr. Ayers said with justifiable exasperation, "ain't I a white man? Can't I kill a native if I want to? I ain't the first man that ever did it, any more than I'm the first man that ever made a mistake. I never meant to do the chap in; it was the bosun I was looking for. He had no business popping out on me so suddenly, before I had time to recognize him. His own bloody fault."

The bosun, having got accustomed to being knocked about by Mr. Ayers, had developed his powers of resistance to where a blow with a bit of wood, such as had done for the luckless Yo Ho, did not faze him at all; he assimilated it as he did labor or typhoons or any other inexplicable act of Fate. But Yo Ho's young and comparatively untried skull was thin and when Mr. Ayers, suffering a mild indigestion, was informed after dinner that a party shifting cargo in the after hold had gone forward to mess and left the hatches off, he knew a red rage. Yo Ho responded in swift alarm to his bellowing and scurried forward after the bosun.

The more Mr. Ayers thought about his stomach and the unclosed hold the madder he got, so taking his short, heavy stick which he humorously called the bosun's wife, he tramped furiously after Yo Ho's fading shape.

The tropical stars swung overhead, swinging slowly about the Diana's masthead; the deck was dark. This was Mr. Ayers' excuse, this was why he felled the first man who appeared in the fo'c's'le doorway. Only this happened to be Yo Ho flitting back to the saloon, where he knew he would be in demand by this time. And thereby hangs a tale, as the fiction writers say.

"So, you see, I couldn't help it," Mr. Ayers reiterated. "I wasn't after him. Fool should have kept clear, or announced himself. You can't blame me for keeping discipline aboard ship, y'know."

The captain only grunted. He combed his beard awhile. "Bury'm soon, mister," he said at last.

"Righto, sir," Mr. Ayers agreed, breathing easier. He raised his voice: "Yo—" He paused sheepishly, recovering himself, remembering.

The chief engineer regarded him with malevolent pleasure. "Ye'll aye fetch yerr ain whusky the noo, mon," he croaked.

And tomorrow brought its own troubles. While Mr. Ayers was making arrangements to bury the messboy at sea a deputation from the fo'c's'le waited on him. They were quite calm about it, no fuss and feathers, too calm in fact. Yo Ho must be buried properly on land. Mr. Ayers tried his usual method of storming and cursing them down, he tried logic, then cajolery. But they were unshaken, and Mr. Ayers, looking at their calm, inscrutable faces, saw something there that gave him to pause. There is something eternal in the East, something resilient and yet rocklike, against which the Westerner's brief thunder, his passionate, efficient methods, are as wind. Yo Ho must be interred in earth. There it ended. Or did it end there? Mr. Ayers, coarsened, surfeited with undisputed domination, with his bland conviction regarding his racial superiority; Mr. Ayers looked from face to quiet face, remote and expressionless as so many idols, and Mr. Ayers felt something cold somewhere within him. He took his problem to the captain.

The captain knew his East. His only reply was to curse Mr. Ayers, the dead messboy, the sea and the entire fabric of a civilization that invented ships and sent men to sea in them, in his native Welsh.

"We'll have to do something soon," Mr. Ayers added, strangely humbled. "He won't keep long in this latitude."

The captain, his beard more explosive than ever, cursed Mr. Ayers again in Welsh. After a while Mr. Ayers, chastened and silent, followed him to the bridge.

Thus it happened that a ship carrying a valuable cargo,

a ship of twelve thousand tons requiring thirty-nine men
to operate her, must change course and run three days
for land in order to put ashore one dead Chinaman. And
it bade fair to become a race in very truth, for, as Mr.
Ayers said, in these latitudes near the line. . . .

Mr. Ayers' chastening lasted overnight. He bolstered
his integrity, sharpened his white man's superiority with
whisky, and the next morning he blustered out on deck,
trying so hard to be his usual self that he overdid it. But
against that wall of contemplative Oriental calm, of pre-
occupation with something far, far older than Mr. Ayers
and his mushroom civilization of a short yesterday, he
knew again a sense of irritating inferiority and uncer-
tainty. And all the time Yo Ho lay forward under a
spread tarpaulin on the fo'c's'le head, ignoring them all.
He didn't care what Mr. Ayers thought about it. Mr.
Ayers repaired to the saloon and had a whisky-and-soda.

The Diana rolled and wallowed on. Days burned
slowly, terrifically overhead; night followed with no
diminution of heat. Mr. Ayers lurked sweating and cursing in his cabin, counting the hours until they could get
rid of the body, until the ship became again a sane world
for a man to inhabit. He'd not have thought doing up
a native would make a man this jumpy, but Yo Ho
seemed to have become a part of him: he was Yo Ho
alive, Yo Ho was himself dead on the fo'c's'le, laughing
at himself. Soon Yo Ho became more than a dream of
Mr. Ayers', and by the captain's order they moved him
aft to the poop deck. These latitudes under the equator,
you know. . . .

The ship sailed on, Yo Ho slept with his fathers in his
own celestial glory; and one night Mr. Ayers, blackguard

though he was, went to the rail and hurled the stick which he humorously called the bosun's wife far, far into the darkness. The ship sailed on.

They raised land at last, and just in time; an island off Cambodia point, the southmost cape of the mainland of Siam. And here again the East raised its implacability bodiless as mist against the West and civilization and discipline. They were all going ashore to put away Yo Ho. The captain contemplated his yellow, impassive crew briefly, then delegated the first and second mates to go along, and retired to his cabin swearing. The chief engineer and one of his henchmen joined the party for the sake of the outing.

There was a village. They procured a bullock and cart from the headman while numberless children, naked and shining as pennies, appeared silently as animals, staring at them without offense, as children. Yo Ho's cousins and friends loaded him into the cart, putting beside him two wicker baskets; and with the four white men walking to windward and the Chinese following behind, the procession set out.

The sun was red and implacable as a furnace mouth; once the beach was behind and they were among great impenetrable trees the heat became terrific. Mr. Ayers looked back at the calm, unsweating Chinese with envy and exasperation, mopping his florid face. They followed docilely, with their eyes bent earthward, trotting, trotting. Mr. Ayers cursed and mounted the cart. If he ever got this bloody business over with! His three companions followed his example, and then the engineer's assistant made a discovery.

"Ow, look 'oo's 'ere," he exclaimed. They looked. In

one of the wicker baskets was food for Yo Ho, and in the other were two bottles of whisky, to be put in his grave with him, lest he wake and hunger, or lest he be too poor to make gifts, as is desirable.

Mr. Ayers felt a qualm: he was really quite unsettled over the whole business. But they soon settled him. As the engineer, breaking again into rare speech, put it: "Wull ye rob me o' ma ain bairn?" stopping his walnut of a face with the bottle neck.

" 'Oo cares for a bloody nytive?" his assistant supported him, drinking in turn.

By the time the second bottle was exhausted they were all singing and shouting. The sun swung lower and hotter, and the jungle was imminent with night complete and impenetrable, like a blanket.

"We'll be needin' more whusky the nicht," the chief interrupted himself to suggest. This was an obvious truth, and they ceased singing to stare at one another.

"Ow, that's orlright," the engineer's satellite assured them, "Freddie's the lad to get whisky for 'is pals, 'ay Bucky?"

"Hell," said Mr. Ayers, "how am I to get whisky in this place?" He looked about at the jungle, and at the narrow slashed pathway. Behind them the Chinese trotted tirelessly.

"Why, 'ow'd you get this?" Mr. Ayers focussed his eyes, staring. "Done in a Chinee, didn't yer?"

Of course. It was quite clear. And there were—Mr. Ayers looked back again—literally thousands of them, trotting, trotting tirelessly.

"I say," said Mr. Ayers suddenly, "pull up a bit, will

you? I'll run back and kill another Chinee; get some more whisky," he explained, leaping to the ground.

"Ho, we'll all kill one," the second mate amended. "Get plenty while we're at it."

They sprang from the cart. The Chinese stopped as suddenly and stood huddled.

"Careful, now," Mr. Ayers hissed for caution. "Don't frighten 'em; might put 'em up a tree, y'know."

The Chinese stood watching them as with simulated carelessness the white men approached them. Then the engineer's assistant, doubtless having his sporting blood up, sprang suddenly forward with a bloodcurdling shout. The other three sprang after him, but too late. The quarry had faded into the trees, silently as a mist. But the pursuers were undaunted. The engineer's henchman howled "Gorn aw'y!" and plunged bellowing after them, and the four whites in the lust of pursuit stumbled and fell and rose again, whooping and shouting through the undergrowth, while ever and anon the assistant engineer's "Gorn aw'y!" rose vainly against the silence of jungle ten thousand years old. But not a Chinese did they find. The quarry had melted away like so many shadows.

Darkness had already fallen when one by one they straggled back to the road. They also drew closer together, hushing their breathing and their voices as the tropic night dropped suddenly as a curtain and great hot stars burst soundlessly almost at their finger tips. Intoxication had gone completely out of them.

They struck matches and examined the road. No tracks: the cart must be between them and the beach. They retraced their way, walking swiftly, following the slashed path in the treetops overhead. One stumbled occasionally and rose cursing, running to join the party again, knowing the hushed terror of nothingness. When at last (after how many hours they knew not) they saw a faint light, they were almost running. It was the village; then they heard surf and saw the pale luminousness of the sea, and the lights of the Diana in slow oscillation.

Something loomed suddenly before them; it was the cart, with the bullock placidly ruminant in the shafts. Mr. Ayers shouted and the bosun's voice in quiet reproof said: "Aw li', Mlissy" from somewhere near his feet. Mr. Ayers struck a match.

The crew squatted placidly about in the dust, courteously waiting the white man's pleasure. The bosun rose and his men followed suit silently as bats.

"Mlissy no come, no go boat," the bosun explained. "Mlissy come now, aw li' go boat."

Mr. Ayers struck another match and looked into the cart, uselessly, for the cart was empty.

Appendix:

Sherwood Anderson *

Fᴏʀ ꜱᴏᴍᴇ ʀᴇᴀꜱᴏɴ people seem to be interested not in what Mr. Anderson has written, but from what source he derives. The greater number who speculate upon his origin say he derives from the Russians. If so, he has returned home, "The Triumph of the Egg" having been translated into Russian. A smaller number hold to the French theory. A cabinetmaker in New Orleans discovered that he resembles Zola, though how he arrived at this I can not see, unless it be that Zola also wrote books.

Like most speculation all this is interesting but bootless. Men grow from the soil, like corn and trees: I prefer to think of Mr. Anderson as a lusty corn field in his native

* This essay first appeared on the book page in the Dallas, Texas, *Morning News* of Sunday, April 26, 1925. It was the second essay in a series which was called "Prophets of the New Age" and was concerned with "the contemporary American writers who . . . represent current tendencies in our literature." James B. Meriwether reprinted it in *The Princeton University Library Chronicle*, Spring, 1957. It is reprinted here with the kind permission of the Dallas *Morning News*. Two corrections of wording have been indicated here, but a few corrections of small typographical errors have been made without indication.

Ohio. As he tells in his own story, his father not only seeded him physically, but planted also in him that belief, necessary to a writer, that his own emotions are important, and also planted in him the desire to tell them to someone.

Here are the green shoots, battling with earth for sustenance, threatened by the crows of starvation; and here was Mr. Anderson, helping around livery stables and race tracks, striping bicycles in a factory until the impulse to tell his story became too strong to be longer resisted.

"Winesburg, Ohio."

The simplicity of this title! And the stories are as simply done: short, he tells the story and stops. His very inexperience, his urgent need not to waste time or paper taught him one of the first attributes of genius. As a rule first books show more bravado than anything else, unless it be tediousness. But there is neither of these qualities in "Winesburg." Mr. Anderson is tentative, self-effacing with his George Willards and Wash Williamses and banker White's daughters, as though he were thinking: "Who am I, to pry into the souls of these people who, like myself, sprang from this same soil to suffer the same sorrows as I?" The only indication of the writer's individuality which I find in "Winesburg" is his sympathy for them, a sympathy which, had the book been done as a full-length novel, would have become mawkish. Again the gods looked out for him. These people live and breathe: they are beautiful. There is the man who organized a baseball club, the man with the "speaking" hands, Elizabeth Willard, middle-aged, and the oldish doctor, between whom was a love that Cardinal Bembo might have dreamed. There is a Greek word for a love like theirs which Mr. Anderson probably had never heard. And behind all of them a ground of fecund earth and corn in the green spring and the slow, full hot summer and the rigorous masculine winter that hurts it not, but makes it stronger.

"Marching Men."

Just as there are lesser ears and good ears among the corn, so are there lesser books and good books in Mr. Anderson's list. "Marching Men" is disappointing after "Winesburg." But then anything any other American was doing at that time would have been disappointing after "Winesburg."

"Windy McPherson's Son."

After reading "A Story Teller's Story," one can see where Windy McPherson came from. And a comparison, I think, gives a clear indication of how far Mr. Anderson has grown. There is in both "Marching Men" and "Windy McPherson's Son" a fundamental lack of humor, so much so that this lack of humor mitigates * against him, but then growing corn has little time for humor.

"Poor White."

The corn still grows. The crows of starvation can no longer bother it nor tear its roots up. In this book he seems to get his fingers and toes again into the soil, as he did in "Winesburg." Here again is the old refulgent earth

* Here the original published version was garbled: ". . . a fundamental lack of humor, so much so that this lack of humor. This lack of humor mitigates . . ."

and people who answer the compulsions of labor and food and sleep, whose passions are uncerebral. A young girl feeling the sweet frightening inevitability of adolescence, takes it as calmly as a tree takes its rising sap, and sees the spring that brought it become languorous and drowsy with summer, its work accomplished.

"Many Marriages."

Here, I think, is a bad ear, because it is not Mr. Anderson. I don't know where it came from, but I do know that it is not a logical development from "Winesburg" and "Poor White." The man here is a factory owner, a bourgeois, a man who was "top dog" because he was naturally forced to run his factory with people who had no factories of their own. In his other books there are no "under dogs" because there are no "top dogs"—save circumstance, your true democracy being at the same time a monarchy. And he gets away from the land. When he does this he is lost. And again humor is completely lacking. A 40-year old man who has led a sedentary life must look sort of funny naked, walking up and down a room and talking. What would he do with his hands? Did you ever see a man tramping back and forth and talking, without putting his hands in his pockets? However, this story won the Dial prize in its year, so I am possibly wrong.

This has been translated into Russian and has been dramatized and produced in New York.

"Horses and Men."

A collection of short stories, reminiscent of "Winesburg," but more sophisticated. After reading this book you inevitably want to reread "Winesburg." Which makes one wonder if after all the short story is not Mr. Anderson's medium. No sustained plot to bother you, nothing tedious; only the sharp episodic phases of people, the portraying of which Mr. Anderson's halting questioning manner is best at. "I'm a Fool," the best short story in America, to my thinking, is the tale of a lad's adolescent pride in his profession (horse racing) and his body, of his belief in a world beautiful and passionate created for the chosen to race horses on, of his youthful pagan desire to preen in his lady's eyes that brings him low at last. Here is a personal emotion that does strike the elemental chord in mankind.

Horses! What an evocative word in the history of man. Poets have used the horse as a symbol, kingdoms have been won by him; throughout history he has been a part of the kings of sports from the days when he thundered with quadrigae, to modern polo. His history and the history of man are intermingled beyond any unraveling; separate both are mortal, as one body they partake of the immortality of the gods. No other living thing holds the same place in the life of man as he does, not even the dog. One sometimes kicks a dog just for the sake of the kick.

Horses are a very part of the soil from which Mr. Anderson came. With horses his forefathers pioneered the land, with horses they wrung and tamed it for corn; bones and sweat of numberless men and horses have helped to make the land fecund. And why shouldn't he (the horse) receive his tithe of the grain he helped to make? Why shouldn't the best of his race know unfettered the arrogance and splendor of speed?

It is well. He, the chosen of his race, becomes, with

the chosen of the race of man, again immortal upon a dirt track: let his duller brethren break ground for the duller among the race of man, let them * draw the wagon to town and back in the late dusk, plodding under the stars. Not for him, gelded and reft of pride, to draw a creaking laden wagon into the barn, not for him to plod sedately before a buggy under the moon, between the fields of corn along the land.

In this book there are people, people that walk and live, and the ancient stout earth that takes his heartbreaking labor and gives grudgingly, mayhap, but gives an hundredfold.

"A Story Teller's Story."

Here Mr. Anderson, trying to do one thing, has really written two distinct books. The first half, which was evidently intended to portray his physical picture, is really a novel based upon one character—his father. I don't recall a character anywhere exactly like him—sort of a cross between the Baron Hulot and Gaudissart. The second half of the book in which he draws his mental portrait is quite different: it leaves me with a faint feeling that it should have been in a separate volume.

Here Mr. Anderson pries into his own mind, in the same tentative manner in which he did the factory owner's mind. Up to here he is never philosophical; he believes that he knows little about it all, and leaves the reader to draw his own conclusions. He does not even offer opinions.

But in this second half of the book he assumes at times an elephantine kind of humor about himself, not at all the

* Here the original has "him."

keen humor with which he pictured his father's character. I think that this is due to the fact that Mr. Anderson is interested in his reactions to other people, and very little in himself. That is, he has not enough active ego to write successfully of himself. That is why George Moore is interesting only when he is telling about the women he has loved or the clever things he has said. Imagine George Moore trying to write "Horses and Men"! Imagine Mr. Anderson trying to write "Confessions of a Young Man"! But the corn is maturing: I think the first half of "A Story Teller's Story" is the best character delineation he has done; but taking the book as a whole I agree with Mr. Llewellyn Powys in the Dial: it is not his best contribution to American literature.

Not Yet Really Mature.

I do not mean to imply that Mr. Anderson has no sense of humor. He has, he has always had. But only recently has he got any of it into his stories, without deliberately writing a story with a humorous intent. I wonder sometimes if this is not due to the fact that he didn't have leisure to write until long after these people had come to be in his mind; that he had cherished them until his perspective was slightly awry. Just as we cherish those whom we love; we sometimes find them ridiculous, but never humorous. The ridiculous indicates a sense of superiority, but to find something partaking of an eternal sardonic humor in our cherished ones is slightly discomforting.

No one, however, can accuse him of lacking in humor in the portrayal of the father in his last book. Which, I think, indicates that he has not matured yet, despite his accomplishments so far. He who conceived this man has yet something that will appear in its own good time.

We were spending a week-end on a river boat, Anderson and I. I had not slept much and so I was out and watching the sun rise, turning the muddy reaches of the Mississippi even, temporarily to magic, when he joined me, laughing.

"I had a funny dream last night. Let me tell you about it," was his opening remark—not even a good morning.

"I dreamed that I couldn't sleep, that I was riding around the country on a horse—had ridden for days. At last I met a man, and I swapped him the horse for a night's sleep. This was in the morning and he told me where to bring the horse, and so when dark came I was right on time, standing in front of his house, holding the horse, ready to rush off to bed. But the fellow never showed up—left me standing there all night, holding the horse."

To blame this man on the Russians! Or anybody else. One of his closest friends called him "the Phallic Checkhov." He is American, and more than that, a middle westerner, of the soil: he is as typical of Ohio in his way as Harding was in his. A field of corn with a story to tell and a tongue to tell it with.

I can not understand our passion in America for giving our own productions some remote geographical significance. "Maryland" chicken! "Roman" dressing! The "Keats" of Omaha! Sherwood Anderson, the "American" Tolstoi! We seem to be cursed with a passion for geographical cliche.

Certainly no Russian could ever have dreamed about that horse.